THOUGHTS
ON MY
THOUGHTS

THOUGHTS
ON MY
THOUGHTS

The <u>TALES</u> That Wagged This Veterinarian

Walter R. Hoge, DVM

Printed in the United States of America
ISBN 978-1-958434-68-0 (sc)
ISBN 978-1-958434-69-7 (hc)
ISBN 978-1-958434-70-3 (e)

Library of Congress Control Number: 2022922117

2022.12.05

MainSpring Books
5901 W. Century Blvd
Suite 750
Los Angeles, CA, US, 90045

www.mainspringbooks.com

Table of Contents

About the Book

In 1952 Stanley L. Miller carried out the Miller-Urey experiment which showed that complex organic molecules could be synthesized from inorganic compounds. This discovery gave a huge boost to the scientific investigation of the origin of life. Indeed, for some time it seemed like the creation of life in a test tube was within reach of experimental science. This "God-like" discovery had a strong influence on the atmosphere in science classes I attended in the 60's. Over the centuries nature and man through natural and man's selection have changed the appearance and productivity of plant and animal life. The life we observe today is much different than seen by earlier civilizations. The laws of natural selection, survival of the fittest and genetic material placed into plant and animal genomes from infections by viruses and bacteria over the eons of time have ensured that the evolution of living matter is a continuing dynamic force. Modern research is also changing life on our world by removing or splicing genetic material in living organisms. These efforts have made it possible to increase food production and nutritional value as well as help prevent or control inherited human diseases.

We have come a long way since Stanley Miller's experiment creating organic building blocks that make up the temporal bodies of the plant and animal kingdom. However, man has never created a living organism from basic matter that makes up the earth and given it the "spark of life" and the ability to regenerate itself. The only documented place I've found where a living organism has been created that could reproduce others of its kind is in Gen 2:7 "then the Lord God formed (that is, created the body of a) man from the dust of the ground, and breathed into his nostrils the breath of life; and the man became a living being (an individual complete in body and spirit)." And, it appears that He also breathed life into the plants and animals. I'm grateful to have had the opportunity of being able to touch some of God's creations during my lifetime and can't wait for the day when I may meet with Him and ask, "Just how did you do that?"

Preface

In 1973 after spending nine years—including three summers in college, graduate school, and veterinary school I began practicing veterinary medicine. I graduated in the top ten percent of my class, passed exams allowing me to practice in several states, and in a little cocky way felt that I was well prepared with current knowledge to be successful in my chosen career. I at first was even a little judgmental of how experienced veterinarians in the field were practicing their trade. However, I soon realized that even though my colleagues maybe were not doing things I had learned in school they were healing their patients, had good communication skills, were respected in the community, successfully running a business, and paying their bills. I soon made it a goal to observe and learn the "art of veterinary practice" my successful peers were using before I developed my practice methods. Over the years I have taken the time to share this learned advice to candidates interviewing for their first job out of veterinary school.

One day I was visiting with a condominium owner in Oakland California who in a joking manner said, "I understand that your business is going to the dogs." I was so into my prideful self from my accomplishments in school that I allowed this statement to offend me. This was the first of many jolts that helped me get off my pedestal of importance and into the reality that if I truly wanted to have joy in my chosen career that it would only come from serving the client in a way that I would like to be served, being prepared to care for the patient with the best standard of care available and being honest with myself that I would not be happy long if I just looked at my job as a job. I am pleased to report that I have been practicing veterinary medicine for forty-eight years and have been at the same location for forty-five years. I've had ups and downs but never considered leaving my career except for two times. One was to care for my kid's mom when she was dying from cancer and she insisted that I could never be very happy if I sold my practice. The other was when I had a stroke and realized that if I were to die that my estate would be mostly tied up in my practice and building which most likely would place financial stress on one of my five children who worked with me. My son and I sold the practice to a corporation, they did not want to keep me on staff because of my stroke, they agreed to let me at least come and care for some of my clients and I have been back to work ever since. Our society talks about burnout and depression—my mind thinks about what a wonderful day in the neighborhood I had visiting with and carry for the needs of clients I've known for years. Over the years I have fortunately missed few days from work and the pattern continues to this day. At my age, I have many a day that I feel tired, a little down, or with aches and pains that I'd rather not face. However, as

I drive home from work I usually have had an uplifting and joyful experience that has stimulated my brain plasticity. I'm currently at work less than usual and find that when I'm away that it's easier to get bored and down some even when I have things to keep me busy.

My youngest son, Jeremy, worked with me for twelve years after graduating from veterinary school. We were known as Dr. Knowledge and Dr. Wisdom. Dr. Knowledge acquired his status by being acquainted with current facts, truths, and principles about veterinary medicine that were primarily gained through books, research, delving into facts, and hands-on experience under the guidance of one possessing knowledge and wisdom. Dr. Wisdom acquired his status of the power of discernment and judging properly as to what is true or right from the attainment of knowledge and experiences acquired over time. Marilyn Vos Savant summarized these thoughts when she wrote, "To acquire knowledge, one must study; but to acquire wisdom, one must observe."

The adventure of writing this book began in the middle of 2010 when one of the leaders in my church assigned me to contact and minister to families that for various reasons were not attending religious services and let him know if they had any special needs. I found that most of these people wished not to be personally visited and, since sending emails or texts was not very personal, in my somewhat bashful way I started writing heartfelt letters that I hoped would be uplifting and of interest to them. I later began sending letters to clients I had become close to that were suffering from medical, aging, lonely or anxiety issues. Lastly, I knew that some of my children would eventually wonder about my thoughts and life experiences and that a journal would most likely never be read. With this in mind, I tried to write about interesting subjects occurring in the world that had influenced my life.

When looking over a career I'm sure most of us at one time or the other wonder if we had ever taken the opportunity to make a difference in anyone's life. It seems like most of my Adams Apple caught in my mouth moist-eyed experiences have come unexpectedly, were not because of my medical or surgical abilities and happened because I took a little extra time listening to the client and letting them know that I did have an interest in them and the struggles they were going through. The song "Have I Done Any Good?" has filtered more often in my mind as my career and life's pace have slowed down.

Included is a letter I received from a client that I do not remember or the events that she refers to. However, it is one of the special moments that unexpectedly from time to time have come my way that have uplifted me in my life and career in a way that fame or fortune alone couldn't ever provide. Hopefully, you will find the experiences I share in "THOUGHTS ON MY THOUGHTS—The Tales That Wagged This Veterinarian" will lift your spirits a bit and help you gain more appreciation for the animal kingdom we share our lives with on this beautiful planet in which we live.

January 26, 2021
Dr. Walter Hoge
Camden Pet Hospital
4960 Camden Ave
San Jose, CA 95124

Dear Dr. Hoge:

I wanted to reach out to you and thank you for everything you have done for me over the years. The last time we spoke was a few years ago when we put our wonderful Yellow lab Jett down. It was such an awful time in my life. I had left my abusive husband of 23 years and took Jett with me. I couldn't leave Jett as my ex-husband had mistreated Jett and threatened to kill him on many occasions.

I rented a condo and the owner made a number of inappropriate advances. When I let him know I was not going to have any kind of a relationship with him, he evicted me. Then I was trying to find another place to live in a short amount of time with a 90-pound lab.

I took Jett to my friends' 60-acre ranch in San Juan Bautista. It was so hard on him. He lived in the house with us and on the ranch, the dogs lived outside in kennels. He was attacked by a raccoon and had a terrible infection on his back. When he recovered from that, he then had diabetes. Of course, then we came to see you. We, my daughter and I, were heartbroken. I know Jett loved to see you and I cannot express my gratitude for your compassion for him when it came time to let him go.

I left all my material possessions in the divorce. My ex-husband threatened to kill me many times and was so afraid I let him have everything. I started over. I met a wonderful man who would not hurt me if his life depended on it. We eventually moved to Shingle Springs, CA (off Hwy 50, 15 minutes before Placerville).

I know the soft spot you have for labs. We have 2, a 13-year-old Chocolate, my step dog, and a 3-year old Yellow. My Yellow, Dexter, completed the CGC AKC program and once COVID restrictions are lifted we plan on working on therapy dog and scent training/games. He'd do well at doc dogs too. He would fetch out of the pool all day if you let him. When we stop throwing, he will throw the ball himself. We live on an acre and have a 200-acre farm. The dogs love it. :)

Stephanie, my daughter, lives in Campbell with her husband, two cats, and a black lab mix. One of her cats is Pickles (Polly Pickles in your records). We adopted her from your office many years ago. They are all fine. You probably won't see her. Her father still lives in the old house close to your office and he was abusive to her as well. She decided to not have a relationship with him and does not want to risk a chance encounter.

Sometimes we don't know the impact we have on others. You made a point to let me know that everything will work out. Your kind words meant the world to me at a time when hope was scarce. I'm semi-retired and have time to appreciate the good things in my life now. Please know you are one of the "good things", thank you.

I quote you often especially to people with young rambunctious dogs "In two years they will settle down". You were so right on that one. I see your son is working in the practice now. That has to be a great thing to see him successful and thriving. I wish you all the happiness and blessings life has to offer.

Kindest regards,
Cindy

"Have I done any good in the world today?
Have I helped anyone in need?
Have I cheered up the sad and made someone feel glad?
If not, I have failed indeed.
Has anyone's burden been lighter today because
I was willing to share? Have the sick and
the weary been helped on their way?
When they needed my help was I there?"
"Have I Done Any Good?"

Music and Lyrics by Will L. Thompson, 1847–190 Walter G. Hoge Thoughts on Walter R. Hoge as a Child "We are shaped and fashioned by what we love." Goethe 1749-1832

My father, the son of a dentist, was raised in the town of Blackfoot Idaho. He played in the high school band for four years, earned a letter in football, and was on the debate team that for two years in a row won the state championship. He played in a dance band during high school and continued playing to help earn money for college until he graduated the first time from BYU in 1936. He had little to no exposure to the animal kingdom until I came on the scene. I remember that dad did not belittle or discourage my interests. He believed that agency to choose was a gift from God and all mankind should be allowed his freedom of choice no matter the outcome. I had the impression that dad would have liked me to follow in his footsteps, but I know as human medicine changed and he saw the opportunities availed me in veterinary medicine he complimented me on my career choice several times in his later years. In the middle of a surgery, my eldest newly married son called me. He was graduating from college with a soon to be awarded accounting degree placed in his pocket and he was trying to decide on a job offer from a firm in Utah and one in California that my Camden Pet Hospital business was a client. He was troubled as to which offer to take and wanted my advice. Wishing with all my heart that he would come to California, I gave him the choice of agency that my father had given me years ago. I suspected at the time that he had a wife that wished to live near her family which weighed heavily on Chris' decision and that a happy wife raises the odds for a happy life. Following his experiences, over the years his family has had a happy life and a successful career.

Reading my father's autobiography several years after his death I have come to appreciate how he accepted the passion I had for animals and the joy I had playing and working with them. I would like to share his thoughts on my life living under his roof:

". . . There is a concrete drive into the garage, chain link fences around the house, and barbed wire around the pasture. By this time the pasture is supporting only several horses, a couple of them are ours and sometimes the Lilyas' (Barbara Ann's family—my sister) bring theirs into pasture for a while. When the children were growing up, we had a variety of animals, mostly Rich's: cows, swine, sheep, chickens, rabbits, Chinese pheasants (from eggs rescued by Rich when some farm machinery about turned the nest over). Rich also brought in fish, polliwogs, fighting cocks, hamsters, a chipmunk, mice, white rats, and, I am sure, a lot of other things. The white rats (added—there were several generations from several rats and a couple of them got loose in the house helping my family make this decision) ended up going to Idaho State University as experimental animals. We only had one dog, Judy, which we all loved, and any number of stray cats that hung around looking for mice but never got inside the house. I am sure all of these animals kept Rich's interest stimulated, finally directing him into veterinary medicine." *Autobiography by Walter Grimmett Hoge, M.D., Born March 13, 1914, Chapter 3, page 23*

While attending an FFA (Future Farmers of America) meeting in Kansas City Kansas my prize New Hampshire sow named Miss Royal Charm the IV was farrowing and having trouble delivering her piglets. My father the M.D. surgeon and general practitioner brought home his sterile obstetrical and gynecology instrument pack in a house call medical bag full of drugs and supplies with sterile gloves. He knelt in a stall full of straw and muck and saved the day by helping Miss Royal Charm IV deliver a fine litter. What more could you ask from a father? If you asked my father, he would have probably mentioned my mother who was raised on a ranch and had a lot of influence on my interest in animals and my father's tolerance of me. Maybe this is a little like the influence my daughter-in-law had on where my son Chris went to work and the born before Christ Athenian statesman Themistocles' comment about his happy wife, happy life deal.

Themistocles (527-460 BCE) was an Athenian statesman and general whose emphasis on naval power and military skills were instrumental during the Persian wars, victory in which ensured that Greece survived its greatest ever threat. He once said jokingly that his son, who was spoiled by his mother and through her by himself, was more powerful than any man in Greece, 'for the Athenians command the Greeks, I command the Athenians, his mother commands me, and he commands her. Themistocles, 95, 527–460 BCE

Most Influencing
Teacher Lovell

As a young lad, I had a New Zealand White doe rabbit that was quite a bit overweight. One day I heard her screaming in her cage and my father and I figured she had broken her back because the rear legs could not lift her. Rabbits reproduce rapidly and are next to plants at the bottom of the food chain, in the sense that rabbits are natural food for any carnivore. They are normally very quiet, can be trained to use a litter box, usually like to be pet, and have a calming effect in the home. Most people would describe a bunny scream as a very loud intensive squeak. Once heard you will never forget the sound. The most common reason why a rabbit screams from intense fear or pain. In the wilds a screaming rabbit usually means it is trying to startle a predator enough to escape. Another fear motivated defense mechanism used by rabbits is laying on their back and looking completely relaxed. This is called "trancing" or "hypnotizing", but it's actually "Tonic Immobility." It is considered to be a fear motivated defense mechanism and the last attempt for the rabbit to escape being eaten. When rabbits are tranced, they are at the highest possible fear level, and they can possibly die from fear.

On my first day starting a new year in middle school the science teacher was going through the class roll, calling each student by name and taking a moment to look at them to see where they were sitting. When he came to my name he stated, "Mr. Hoge stand up." And I quickly did! He proceeded to tell me that he understood I was a disruptive student and liked to fool around. He then told me in no uncertain terms that if I acted up in any way in his class that I would be dismissed immediately and never asked back. He caught me off guard and I was floored. If I were a rabbit in front of the class I would have screamed and gone into a state of "Tonic Immobility" in hopes I could safely find a dark corner or a hole to hide in. To me, I considered this particular year of school high stakes—I had just gotten on the basketball team, and to stay on the team I needed to keep my nose clean and maintain good grades. To make matters worse, science was one of my favorite subjects and I wanted to be in his class.

Rabbits are considered to be a biological "refrigerator" because the meat from one animal can be consumed without storage. They breed year-round and you only need a few animals to provide a steady meat supply. A doe can produce five to six litters a year and an average litter is seven to eight kits, so you can expect 35-40 rabbits per doe per year. Rabbits are butchered at eight to twelve weeks of age and rabbit meat is all-white meat. Domestic rabbits of the variety raised for meat around the world originated from

European wild rabbits. The first recorded rabbitry was in early Roman times, where rabbits were kept and raised in walled gardens for a food supply. In the depression, people fed their rabbits on grass clippings & lived on the meat for an abundant and thrifty source of protein. During World War II civilians were encouraged to include rabbits as a component of their victory gardens. Rabbit meat has fewer calories, the highest percentage of protein, and the lowest of fat and cholesterol of any normally consumed meat. Research shows that rabbit meat has been recommended for special diets such as for heart disease patients, diets for the elderly, low sodium diets, and weight reduction diets. Because it is easily digested, it has been recommended by doctors for patients who have trouble eating other meats.

When my children were young I raised rabbits using yard and garden waste plus a commercially prepared feed. Rabbit raising stopped when my oldest child walked around the corner of the house and observed me preparing one for dinner. That was the end of my family having a rabbit on the menu at my house.

In the 1970s, researchers set up an experiment to examine the effects of diet on heart health. Over several months, they fed a control group of rabbits a high-fat diet and monitored their blood pressure, heart rate, and cholesterol. As expected, many of the rabbits showed a buildup of fatty deposits on the inside of their arteries. Yet this was not all! Researchers had discovered something that made little sense. Although all of the rabbits had a buildup, one group surprisingly had as much as 60 percent less than the others. It appeared as though they were looking at two different groups of rabbits. To scientists, results like this can cause lost sleep. How could this be? The rabbits were all the same breed from New Zealand, from a virtually identical gene pool. They each received equal amounts of the same food. What could this mean?

Did the results invalidate the study? Were there flaws in the experiment design? The scientists struggled to understand this unexpected outcome! Eventually, they turned their attention to the research staff. Was it possible that researchers had done something to influence the results? As they pursued this, they discovered that every rabbit with fewer fatty deposits had been under the care of one researcher. She fed the rabbits the same food as everyone else. But, as one scientist reported, "she was an unusually kind and caring individual." When she fed the rabbits, "she talked to them, cuddled and petted them . . . 'She couldn't help it. It's just how she was.'"

She did more than simply give the rabbits food. She gave them love! At first glance, it seemed unlikely that this could be the reason for the dramatic difference, but the research team could see no other possibility. So, they repeated the experiment—this time tightly controlling for every other variable. When they analyzed the results, the same thing happened! The rabbits under the care of the loving researcher had significantly higher health outcomes.

The scientists published the results of this study in the prestigious Science journal. Years later the findings of this experiment still seem influential in the medical community.

In recent years, Dr. Kelli Harding published a book titled *The Rabbit Effect* that takes its name from the experiment. Her conclusion: "Take a rabbit with an unhealthy lifestyle. Talk to it. Hold it. Give it affection . . . The relationship made a difference . . . Ultimately," she concludes, "what affects our health in the most meaningful ways has as much to do with how we treat one another, how we live, and how we think about what it means to be human."

Mr. Lovell's approach for me, who was developing an unhealthy behavior, was to talk to me in such a way that it had a real impact on me. He held his values as a teacher and showed his affection by helping me succeed in his class. The relationship he established with me made a difference. What I needed was a good look in the mirror at my actions and to decide what course I wanted to follow. I received a good science foundation under Mr. Lovell's guidance and my grades in all courses began to improve as I continued studies through high school. Fortunately, my ACT scores qualified my attending the University of Idaho and then on to Purdue University for a Master's Degree and then veterinary school. In both universities I had been well prepared for their science curriculum partly from the effort Mr. Lovell made in class plus helping wake me up to the reality that getting attention through foolishness would not get me to where I wanted to be.

Dr. Harding uses the rabbit study to introduce the more profound ideas that both rabbits and people can thrive in a community, that health is bolstered by "love, connection, and purpose," and that kind treatment, in general, can modify health on a molecular, individual, interpersonal, and global level. The Rabbit Effect: Live Longer, Happier, and Healthier with the Groundbreaking Science of Kindness, Dr. Helland is a Resident in Psychiatry, Montefiore Medical Center, Bronx, NY

"There is beauty all around When there's love at home; There is joy in every sound When there's love at home; Peace and plenty here abide, Smiling sweet on every side, Time doth softly, sweetly glide, When there's love at home." *Love at Home, John H. McNaughton, 1854, arr. by John D. Brunk, 1904*

The Blackfoot Idaho
Insane Asylum

When I was in high school I worked for a mental hospital (State Hospital South— SHS, Blackfoot Idaho). It was established in 1883 before Idaho became a state when the Territorial Legislation authorized building the Idaho Insane Asylum. Before 1889, rocks were mined and patients, called inmates, and employees used them to make bricks. They were used for making buildings. In earlier years, patients were given SHS tokens for their labor. These tokens could be used to purchase items at the Canteen and Country Store at the hospital. The hospital's farm included over 3,000 acres of land, 22 acres of orchards with at least 1,500 fruit trees, a dairy, a cannery, a slaughterhouse, and an apiary for 90 hives of bees. The SHS farm was so productive that it also provided food to State Hospital North, Idaho State School, and Hospital and the territorial prison in Boise. An A-grade dairy provided all of the needs of the patients and staff. The farm was the focus of the institutional culture until it was abandoned in the early 1960s. From 1946 to 1947 there were 7,000 insulin, which is used to control diabetics, shock treatments (comas induced by high doses of insulin) that were used extensively in the 1940s and 1950s, mainly for depression, before falling out of favor and being replaced by neuroleptic drugs in the 1960s. SHS was a pioneer research site in 1953 for the development of Chlor-Promazine (Thorazine). It was the first major antipsychotic drug. Also, during 1946-1947 there were 2,400 electroconvulsive treatments (ECT) performed primarily to treat depression at Blackfoot's State Hospital South by a neurologist and neurosurgeon. With ECT, electrodes are placed on the patient's scalp and a finely controlled electric current is applied while the patient is under general anesthesia. The current causes a brief seizure in the brain. ECT is currently being used when other types of therapy are not successful. It is one of the fastest ways to relieve symptoms in severely depressed or suicidal patients. It's also very effective for patients who suffer from mania or several other mental illnesses.

As a senior in high school, I wanted to get some medical experience. My early thoughts on a career included medical school, teaching & research, or veterinary medicine. Knowing my father (an MD in town) the State Hospital South made certain that I was exposed to all aspects of medicine. On my first day on the job, I helped hold a man for spinal taps who was inflicted with Syphilis. I will always remember how warm the room seemed to get and the thought that I might faint as I watched and felt the crying out of the man as they attempted time and again to collect a fluid sample from his spinal canal. I learned a lot about mental illness, the uses of medications, to keep sharp objects (even a small covered razor blade) from my charges, the process of dying and cleaning the dead before they were removed from the hospital, why we kept the patients separated from the opposite sex and that no matter how much progress a patient seemed to be making there could be a complete set back before I reported to work for my next shift.

I was also allowed to help with electroconvulsive treatments (ECT). The patient was given a short anesthetic or none (results were often greater with an awake patient), two electrodes were placed on the skull and a short burst of electricity passed through the brain. In preparation the patient's legs and arms were strapped to the table, a protective mouthguard inserted between the teeth and the head secured so that they would not injure themselves. The electricity caused the patient to become stiff (similar to an epileptic seizure) for several seconds. As they came out of the effects of the shock they would begin thrashing around, more violently at first, until relaxation and consciousness returned. My task was to help prevent injury during the recovery period. ECT was used for depression and despite the process, I saw a lot of people helped using the therapy. My grandmother Sarah Louise Hoge's 59-year-old husband, Walter Smith Hoge, was killed on December 1, 1940, from accidental gunshot wounds while on a geese hunting trip. He had returned to the car to reload his shotgun and a shell discharged that tore through his left shoulder. His companions found him approximately ½ hour later, rushed him to Blackfoot where he died from blood loss. I have his shotgun, never have used it, and noticed when my dad gave it to me that there was a new stock on the gun. Dad has never said anything, but I have always suspected he broke the stock in anger while grieving the death of his father. After many years, living mostly alone as a widower, grandmother was treated for depression with ECT and made a good recovery. The only bad thing was that dad, being one of the few doctors in our small community, had to endure my recovered grandmother who felt so good that she ran for city council in Blackfoot. Her campaign slogan was "fixing the cracks in the sidewalks of Blackfoot". Dad was quite embarrassed about the whole thing and grandma almost won the election. I have always had the impression that dad made some phone calls and maybe spent some bucks to help grandma get defeated. Grandma had in earlier years helped establish a park and building the Blackfoot swimming pool.

Attending the University of Idaho, I had a catfish for a pet. One day I was walking back to my dorm room after lunch and the lights in the hallway flickered several times but did not go out. Upon entering my room, I noticed my catfish floating belly up in the fishbowl. After several seconds it started swimming in circles upside down, then it began to gain its balance and eventually began swimming and acting normal. What my roommates had done was bare the wires on an extension cord, held a tip in the water on each side of the fishbowl, and plugged the cord into an electric outlet electrocuting the catfish. They performed ECT on my pet fish!

Rumor had it that when the ECT machine was purchased by the hospital in Blackfoot the psychiatrists tried it on themselves before using it on the patients. It impressed me that they were so dedicated to their work that they would risk their health before trying it out on others. However, I was not impressed with my classmates and their experiment on my fish.

I remember reading an article about a veterinarian who was curious enough to understand the life cycle of the ear mite and its effects on dogs and cats that he placed in his ears and monitored how he felt. He would record when they were the most active (mostly at night), how they interrupted his activities, and the amount of inflammation and wax produced in his ears. He then treated himself as he would a dog or a cat to cure the disease. This study gave at least me a lot of insight into the parasite and I think he was a real scientist (somewhat like an astronaut) for doing such a thing. During the early 1980's Dr. Barry Marshall was convinced that human ulcers were caused by a bacteria called H. pylori. After failed attempts to infect piglets in 1984, Marshall, after having a baseline endoscopy done, drank a petri dish containing the cultured H. Pylori, and expected to develop, perhaps years later, an ulcer. He was surprised when only three days later, he developed vague nausea and due to lack of acid in the stomach, the waste products of the bacteria caused halitosis. On day eight, he had a repeat endoscopy and biopsy, which showed massive inflammation (gastritis), and H. Pylori was cultured. On the fourteenth day after ingestion, a third endoscopy was done, and Marshall began to take antibiotics. This story is related by Berry Marshall himself in his Nobel acceptance lecture on Dec. 8, 2005, and the experiment was published in 1985 in the 'Medical Journal of Australia' and is among the most cited articles from the journal. Here again what a scientist. He placed his health and safety on the line to test a theory that has made it possible to treat ulcers with antibiotics and saved many from suffering.

The State Hospital South floors were separated into wards. Two of the floors contained resident patients and orderlies separated by sex. We were instructed to keep the occupants of each floor separate at all times. When our ward went to dinner or organized activities it was always scheduled when each group could be separated. If anyone from the opposite sex entered a ward there had to be at least two of them together while on that ward. At times when things got out of hand on the women's floor men orderlies would be called down to assist. One incident I will never forget was when a young woman was out of control. Us orderlies were trying to place her in a safe room where she would receive medication and be placed in restraints to help prevent her from injuring herself. As we arrived on the woman's floor I could hear screaming and people in loud voices trying to calm her. Getting closer to the patient I noticed a nice-looking middle-aged woman that was missing all of her clothes. For a young man approaching 18 years of age, this was a very new and psychologically shocking experience. When we assembled with the other orderlies and nurses to establish a "plan of action", suddenly the young out of control woman looked at me and said, "There you are my honey." She then came to me, placed her arm in mine, and with her nice-looking God-given gifts in full display let me escort her to the safe room. As I left her and started back to the upper men's ward my manhood felt complimented that she sent her attention my way, embarrassed at what I had seen, and had some aroused thoughts that would best not be in a 17-year old's brain. About 132 years later State Hospital South is still caring for patients on 700 E. Alice Street in Blackfoot Idaho. Diseases are mostly the same but treatments and medication have changed over the years.

The events I've seen during my life leads me to believe just what the good book says—the only thing that has never changed in the past, present, or future is—God.

In a class during my sophomore year in high school, I noticed a girl, who I knew by name only, looking at me from across the room. It happened several times over two weeks and I finally asked some of my buddies if they knew much about her. Her name was Sheryl Gardner and I noticed that she was an attractive girl especially when I noticed her in gym gear playing volleyball. We became friends and the next class term we sat next to each other in typing class. I stupidly tried to better her in the class and proved a fool when it came to typing. I found out she had enough self-control that if I wanted to do any fun stuff with her it was homework and home duties first. That attitude helped my grade point average to jump up several notches. One thing that she would not compromise on with her parents and I quote, "If you want me to go to church on Sunday, I'm going to ride my horse on Sunday." Come summer I started working for her father on his farm moving sprinkler pipe, cutting, baling, and hauling hay. Harvest found me bagging peas, rolling over the potato vines before digging, and at times helping feed the livestock. I worked for him during high school and several summers when I returned from college.

For Christmas my junior year in high school I gave Sheryl a gift that on the box alluded that it was a "diamond." All the family gathered around as she opened the gift. As she opened the box there was a hiss and a string pulled the head of a rubber "diamond" back rattlesnake coming at her out of the box. The word snake to a farmer that worked in the desert area in Idaho is like yelling fire in a theater. The bewilderment as to why a high school friend would give her a hopefully not ring turned to why would he pull such a trick especially on Christmas Eve. Sheryl's little sister, Peggy, grabbed the gift and threw it into the fire. The smell of burning rubber filled the air and "even though I tried not to show it, I really was quite pleased with myself."

A cousin whose name I will not put in print, borrowed a wedding ring from a jewelry store when the owner wasn't looking in Boise Idaho. This occurred during a 4H conference. His mother was the county agent of Bingham County Idaho and was conducting the event. During the spring of my senior year, I borrowed the ring and with my best friend laying behind the front seat of the car found a good place to park in front of her house and played a less dangerous home version of the game we teenagers called watching the "submarine races." I proposed to her and we were going through a long conversation as to why we should not at this time in our lives get married. She told me that we were going to the University of Idaho in the fall and that neither one of us had the ways, means, or money to do such a stupid thing. About that time my friend started cracking up behind the front seat and could not stop laughing. "I again tried not to show it, but I really was quite pleased with myself." As for the ring—one of our friends had the misfortune of getting a girl pregnant (probably playing the more dangerous parked in the woods at the gravel pits version of watching the "submarine races") while still in high school and my cousin gave the ring to him so he would at least have one for the wedding.

At the University of Idaho, I enrolled in their animal science department and took classes in what was called animal science, science. I took the same classes as the pre-medical and dental students. The only difference was that the electives for them were general literature and artsy-type stuff. As for me, my electives were beef, horse, sheep, and pig production; meats—like a butcher learns, practicum—knowing very little about sheep, I won a ribbon from one that I prepared and showed for the event, class on the history of the State of Idaho and all the rest I can't remember. One event I do remember was a class where we did assignments giving us a feeling of what graduate school and research would be like. One of the experiments was getting an object to be expelled into a hen's egg. So, when you cracked open the egg an item would be found amongst the yolk and albumin. Sheryl had an engagement ring on her finger but I had possession of the wedding band. You guessed it. I wanted to get that wedding band into a gift-wrapped box that she would never forget—an egg.

The reproductive system of the female chicken is in two parts: the ovary and oviduct. Unlike most female animals, which have two functioning ovaries, the chicken usually has only one. The right ovary stops developing when the female chick hatches, but the left one continues to mature. The ovary contains a cluster of follicles just like most other animals and man. Instead of shedding small eggs from the follicles for fertilization, the hen sheds the yellowish/orange yolk one sees when an egg is cracked. The yolk breaks away from the ovary and slides into a funnel-shaped tube, called the oviduct, and passes down the tube into the uterus where the yolk and a secretion of the protein albumin are surrounded with a hard material called a shell. In most animals that are not birds, fish or reptiles the uterus is where the offspring is incubated until it is mature enough to be born. After an egg is laid another yolk is released from the ovary.

I couldn't wait for lab day and the opportunity to do surgery on a living organism. Getting Sheryl's wedding band into that egg would be another event that, "I would not try to show it, but I really would be quite pleased with myself." I fully intended to put the wedding band into the oviduct of a chicken and see if she would lay an egg with the ring in it. However, a clearer head told me that I should try the experiment first and see if it would be reliable enough to place an expensive, to me, wedding gift into a live chicken. Most of my classmates didn't put anything of much value in the oviduct, I don't remember what I used—but I did not use the ring. I checked my hen for several days and she did not pass the foreign object I had planted in her oviduct. In fact, she never laid another egg. If I had placed the ring inside of that hen I would have had to sacrifice (word used in research meaning kill) the hen and search the entrails for the wedding band. So, again "I did not try to show it, but I really was quite pleased with myself."

And by the way, the guy Sheryl was looking at in class when I first noticed her. She was not looking at me. The guy, Allan Packer the other doctor's son, was sitting where her line of sight scanned both of us. And to my good fortune—Allan was clueless that she was looking at him.

Procrastinate or Straightway

I n 2014 Marvin Ashton commented, "A few weeks ago I was visiting in a faraway country with a discouraged missionary. When I asked, 'How long has it been since you wrote a letter to your mother?' he said, 'Oh, about three or four weeks, I guess.' When I suggested he write her a letter straightway, he responded with, 'What does straightway mean?' Straightway is a power word. Straightway is an action word. It means immediately, without delay or hesitation. It means at once. Also, it is associated with having no curve or turn—a straight course, track, or path. Procrastination would be the very opposite of straightway. To procrastinate is to put off intentionally and habitually something that should be done. Procrastination is an unproductive delay. Someone has wisely said, 'Procrastination is a silly thing, it only makes me sorrow, but I can change at any time—I think I will tomorrow!'" *Marvin Ashton, Oct 2014, General Conference.*

During studies at the University of Idaho in the early 1960s, I was much like the young missionary who asked, "What does straightway mean?" My mother would often send me a nice note with a little bit of spending money. However, besides at times sending back corrected letters I had sent home, there was usually this comment at the end of her note with a P.S., "Remember to send your grandma a note about your studies." I was putting off intentionally and habitually something that should be done. Finally, out of the constant bugging from mom and feelings of guilt, I composed a short note and dropped it into the mailbox. A few days later I was informed that Grandma Hoge had passed and I flew home for the funeral. A couple of weeks passed and back on campus the letter I had sent to Grandmother Hoge was returned to me. A big red X had been placed over the address with a note that stated, "deceased—return to sender." That event was an awakening of something I had always known—push anything down line long enough and a time will come when you can't make amends. A poet set to verse the sorrow of opportunities forever lost:

Around the corner, I have a friend,
In this great city that has no end;
Yet days go by, and weeks rush on,
And before I know it, a year is gone,
And I never see my old friend's face,
For Life is a swift and terrible race . . .
But to-morrow comes—and to-morrow goes,
And the distance between us grows and grows.
Around the corner!—yet miles away . . .
"Here's a telegram, sir,"
"Jim died to-day." And that's what we get,
and deserve in the end:

Around the corner, a vanished friend. Charles Hanson Towne,
"Around the Corner,"
in Poems That Live Forever, (1965), 128

I had an experience in high school that should have helped curtail procrastination for the rest of my life. One of my English teachers, Mrs. Allen, was known in private circles as "Old Lady Allen." She was a tough teacher and didn't put up with much. In the long run, having this teacher resulted in an experience that helped me get my "life in order." Most members of her class probably don't remember the poem, "Abou Ben Adhem", as well as I do. We were instructed to memorize the poem and recite it in front of the class. If you gave it correctly the first time the grade received would be an "A", next time "B" etcetera on down to an "F". My next scheduled attempt was to receive a "D" and I figured that a "D" or an "F" wouldn't make much difference. During lunch in the cafeteria a day before my next try Mrs. Allen grabbed and placed me up against the wall in front of the gawking students and said, "The grade does matter and you will recite Abou Ben Adhem perfectly tomorrow in my classroom." And guess what, I did just what she said and I can still recite it in near perfection to this day. She and my mother didn't accept sloppy work or underperformance if they knew that I could complete a task. This lesson has helped me numerous times to not procrastinate, do my best, and complete assignments. I have a bit of anxiety and can't get tasks off my mind until they are completed. She helped give me the extra kick I needed at a good time in my youth. *Walter R. Hoge, 03-21-2014.* Opportunities are perishable. The teacher or parent who procrastinates the pursuit of his or her responsibility as a teacher may, in years to come, gain bitter insight into Whittier's expression: "Of all sad words of tongue or pen, The saddest are these: "It might have been!" Unfortunately, many people procrastinate their future, dread responsibility, and try their best to justify their behavior. How often have we said or heard someone say, "What I do is my business?" But is it? There is a story about a young unmarried woman who protested her parents' interference in her drug addiction on the ageold grounds that what she did with her life was her own business. But when her child was born already dependent on drugs, her irresponsibility was also the business of her child. The consequences of our actions are always felt by those around us. *J. Spencer Kinard, "The Spoken Word," June 3, 1973*

. Abou Ben Adhem

Abou Ben Adhem (may his tribe increase!) "And is mine one?", "Nay, not so,

Awoke one night from a deep dream of peace, Replied the Angel, Abou spoke more low,

And saw, within the moonlight in his room But cheerily still; and said, "I pray thee, then

Making it rich, and like a lily in bloom Write me as one who loves his fellow men."

An Angel writing in a book of gold:

The Angel wrote, and

vanished. The next night

Exceeding peace had made Ben Adhem bold, It came again

with a great wakening light,
And to the Presence in the room he said, And showed the
names whom love of God had blessed,
"What writest thou?" The Vision raised its head, And, lo!
Ben Adhem's name led all the rest!
And with a look made of all sweet accord,
Answered, "The names of those who love the Lord." By
Leigh Hunt (1784-1859) American Clergyman

The returned letter I sent to my Grandmother Hoge had enough of an effect on me that I have kept it in my possession over the years as a reminder that there is a time when you can't make up for the lost time. I still haven't ventured opening it. I'm quite sure I would be disappointed in my attempt to let my grandmother know how much I cared for her and appreciated things she had done for me. "Think of all the years passed by in which you said to yourself "I'll do it tomorrow," and how the gods have again and again granted you periods of the grace of which you have not availed yourself. It is time to realize that you are a member of the Universe, that you are born of Nature itself, and to know that a limit has been set to your time." The last of "Five Good Emperors," *Marcus Aurelius ruled Rome from AD 161 to 180.*

A Child Is Born

D uring graduate school at Purdue University, my NIH (National Institute of Health) grant was to study reproductive hormones and a toxic fungus called ergot. Ergotism is a small organism that attacks developing grass and grain (rye is the worst) type seeds. It forms masses of blackish-brown fungal hyphal material in the developing seed that contains the toxic chemicals that if ingested can cause illness in both animals and man. Ergotism is especially bad during wet growing seasons and when eaten by livestock or one of us folks can result in symptoms including tremors, delusions, prickling sensations on the skin, convulsing seizures, hallucinations, violent muscle spasms, sloughing of skin near the fingers, toes and ear tips, miscarriages, death, and it affects the pituitary gland's reproductive hormone secretions. In fact, it is believed that ergotism had a role in Russia's failed attempt to capture several seaports in 1772 from Turkey, the French revolution in 1789, and the witchcraft trials throughout Europe and colonial America. Ergot toxicity was of interest in our studies because of its ability to affect the pituitary gland's production of prolactin. *Bob Harveson—Extension*

Plant Pathologist, Panhandle Research and Extension Center, 08/17/2017.

The work was interesting: giving anesthetics, dissecting pituitary glands from the base of the brain, placing grafts of pituitary and muscle tissue under the kidney capsule, and evaluating the effects of different compounds on the reproductive structures of rats. What I came away understanding was there are multiple effects that a small amount of hormone can have on a living organism. "Factors Affecting the Secretion Rate of Prolactin by Ectopic Pituitary Tissue", *Walter Rich Hoge, Master's Degree Thesis, Purdue University, 1970.*

I completed my master of science degree in 1970 during my first year of veterinary school. Because of my research experience, I was asked to teach my classmates the physiology lab portion on reproduction. At the time there were no over-the-counter pregnancy tests available. However, during this class, my wife, Sheryl, was diagnosed by her doctor as being pregnant and with a lot of persuasion she agreed to donate some of her urine for the lab I was teaching about pregnancy hormones. If you were an adult in the 1960's you probably remember the phrase, "she was tested and it killed the rabbit." That meant there was a very elated or disappointed young man involved. If she had been given a pregnancy test most likely a rabbit had been used for the diagnosis and had been sacrificed (killed) on her behalf. Dr. M. X. Zarrow had taught me how to run the tests during a class in experimental endocrinology. There were three tests: urine from a suspected pregnant woman was injected into a rabbit or a mouse or a frog. The rabbit and mouse were later sacrificed and their ovaries examined. A positive test for a frog was finding the male frog attaching himself on top of a female frog.

Dr. Zarrow was fairly short in stature, soft-spoken with a panhandle mustache that he stroked often and his eyes looked rather mischievous. One day in the lab, with a beaker of urine placed in front of us fellow graduate students, he lectured on the history of diabetes and the devastating effects it can have on the body of both man and animals. He then led us on a meandering story of the history of the discovering of diabetes and how the sweet taste of a diabetic's urine was conclusive evidence that the person had the disease. He explained that some of the beakers of urine in front of us were from a diabetic and we were to determine if that urine was contained in our beaker. He did it in such a way that nearly all of us dedicated graduate students, including me, were ready to lift our beakers to our mouths and taste the urine. At the climax of his lecture, he gestured towards the beakers as if we should taste the urine and at a well-planned moment mentioned in a soft voice as I remember, "you can taste this sample of urine or you can place this small strip of paper into the beaker of urine to test for sugar." *"Experimental Endocrinology", A Sourcebook of Basic Techniques, Zarrow et al, 1964.*

Five years later a practicing veterinarian and a wife at the nesting time of her life found ourselves childless after having several unsuccessful pregnancies. We were undergoing infertility studies, having no luck with an adoption agency and legal abortions were just getting into full swing in our country. During an office visit with our fertility physician he mentioned that there was the possibility that one of his patients was going to give up her baby at birth for adoption, he felt that the child would be a good fit for our family, he had not delivered a white baby that was adopted in a long time and were we interested. We thought about it for about 0.02 seconds and said we were very interested if the child became available. In our minds, we felt that even if blood is thicker than water we are all God's children and that's where all our blood came from. It should not matter who raises us. What is important is that a child should be raised in a safe loving home, understand what it means to be a good citizen, and have some concept of who they are, why they are here, and develop a spirit of joy during their life. We discussed it at home and reassured ourselves that adoption would be great. But we had had so many false starts and disappointments we weren't going to get our hopes up or prepare more than we had. As I remember, my wife's only stated concern was that she felt it might be harder trying to raise a boy.

While at work examining a dog my receptionist interrupted me, which is normally a no-no, mentioning that a man called and was persistently and forcefully asking to speak with me! In a somewhat irritated demeanor, I answered the phone. It was our fertility doctor. He said that our baby boy had been delivered, did I want him circumcised and if I didn't pick him up the next day the baby would be given to someone else. Looking back at this conversion I suspect the doctor had a good time informing me about the birth. The next day found my wife and me waiting, in our car at a curb in front of a hospital, for adoption paperwork to be done. After what seemed like an hour we were presented with our hopefully to be adoptive son, a diaper, a bottle with warmed formula, and directions stating that we needed to schedule a new baby checkup in 6 weeks.

During my life and career as a veterinarian, I have watched animals instantly bond to their offspring as they were being born. I will never forget, as a teenager, a trip to Yellowstone Park taking pictures of a cow moose and her two calves. Almost unfortunately for me, I got between the mom and her calves. She suddenly came towards me and I luckily had time to beat her to my car. I have always had a hard time putting into words the feelings I had as we left the curb in front of the hospital and started home with our hopefully soon-to-be adopted son. But I can tell you this, "I could not turn onto the freeway before I stopped the car at another curb. With tears in my eyes, I felt a warmth I've felt few times during my life. I took him from my wife's arms and gave him a hug and a kiss on his forehead." The bonding to him was instant and from then on if he has a need I am ready to react as that cow moose did so many years before.

During April of 2021 Elder Neil L. Andersen related his family's experience with the adoption of a child. "In our family, we have been immeasurably blessed as two decades ago, a young 16-year-old learned that she was expecting a child. She and the baby's father were not married, and they could see no way forward together. The young woman believed the life she was carrying was precious. She gave birth to a baby girl and allowed a righteous family to adopt her as their own. For Bryce and Jolinne, she was an answer to their prayers. They named her Emily and taught her to trust in her Heavenly Father and in His Son, Jesus Christ. Emily grew up. How grateful we are that Emily and our grandson, Christian, fell in love and were married in the house of the Lord. Emily and Christian now have their own little girl.

Emily recently wrote: "Throughout these last nine months of pregnancy, I had time to reflect on the events [of] my own birth. I thought of my birth mother, who was just 16 years old. As I experienced the aches and changes that pregnancy brings, I couldn't help but imagine how difficult it would have been at the young age of 16 . . . The tears flow even now as I think of my birth mother, who knew she couldn't give me the life [she desired for me and unselfishly placed] me for adoption. I can't fathom what she might have gone through in those nine months—being watched with judging eyes as her body changed, the teen experiences she missed, knowing that at the end of this labor of motherly love, she would place her child into the arms of another. I am so thankful for her selfless choice, that she did not choose to use her agency in a way that would take away my own." Emily concludes, "I'm so thankful for Heavenly Father's divine plan, for my incredible parents who (loved and cared for) me, and for temples where we can be sealed to our families for eternity."

As I shared this story with my son Chris I related to him that Emily's story best expressed the feelings I have had about his becoming a member of our family. His birth mother was 16 years old, under similar circumstances and we were married in the house of the Lord. Before his mother signed a release to allow the adoption she and his father requested to see their son. It was a very special moment. While the father held back, she held her son and after a short time, he turned his attention to my wife and wanted her to take him. His mother returned him to my wife and she seemed satisfied that her child would be okay. I felt as Emily expressed, "I can't imagine how difficult it would have been at the young age of 16 . . . I am so thankful for her selfless choice, that she did not choose to use her agency in a way that would take away my own." *Elder Neil L. Andersen, Quorum of the Twelve apostles, April 2021, General Conference.*

On Wednesday, December 24th, 1975 Sheryl and I had an appointment to visit with a judge and finalize our son Christopher's adoption. At that time my wife was expecting a baby in April and instinctively wore a long coat that covered up the pregnancy as best she could. There was the fear that if she were pregnant the judge may have denied our request for the adoption. As we walked into the judge's office I extended my hand and he shook it in his left hand. He did not have a right hand. Our anxiety mounted as we sat down. With a pregnant wife and an embarrassing handshake where was this all headed? The judge sat down and spent some time talking about what it means to be a family, our commitment, and how a child in the home would change our lives. He then surprisingly mentioned how pleased he was that he was able to finalize an adoption on Christmas Eve. Then he related a sad story about a couple he had just visited with that were giving up their children.

Sheryl and I were eventually blessed with five children. On came off the shelf and four were home-brewed. Their ages are within five and one-half years of each other. Yup, we went doggy style and raised a litter of kids. And, we have choice memories of how it all started. A son with the name Christopher, which means bearing Christ, and finalization of his adoption on Christmas Eve. Who would of thunk it?

A number of years ago a seminary professor was vacationing with his wife in Gatlinburg, Tennessee where they were eating breakfast at a little restaurant, hoping to enjoy a quiet family meal. While they were waiting for their food, they noticed a distinguished-looking, whitehaired man moving from table to table visiting with the guests. The professor leaned over and whispered to his wife that he hoped the man would not come their way. But sure enough, the man did come over to their table and asked where they were from and how great it was to have them visiting Tennessee. When he found out the professor taught seminary he stated, "Oh, you teach preachers how to preach? Well, I've got a really great story for you." And with that, the gentleman pulled up a chair and sat down at the table with the couple. Pointing his finger towards the base of a mountain out of the restaurant window he stated that there was a boy born there to an unwed mother. He had a hard time growing up, because every place he went, he was always asked where his daddy was. He would hide at recess and lunchtime from other students. He would avoid going into stores because that question hurt him so bad. When he was about 12 years old, a new preacher came to his church. The boy would always go in late and slip out early to avoid being asked who his daddy was. But one day, the new preacher said the benediction so fast he got caught and had to walk out with the crowd. Just about the time, he got to the back door, the new preacher not knowing anything about him, put his hand on his shoulder and asked him who his daddy was. The whole church got deathly quiet. He could feel every eye in the church looking at him. This new preacher, though, sensed the situation around him and using discernment that only the Holy Spirit could give. He told the scared little boy to wait a minute. I know who your daddy is. I see the family resemblance now. You are a child of God. He patted the boy on his shoulder and mentioned that the boy had a great inheritance. With that, the boy smiled for the first time in a long time and walked out the door a changed person. He was never the same again. Whenever anybody asked him who his daddy was he would reply that he was a child of God. The distinguished gentleman got up from the table and the professor mentioned that it was a great story. As the man turned to leave, he said, "You know, if that new preacher hadn't told me that I was one of God's children, I probably never would have amounted to anything!" And he walked away. The seminary professor and his wife were stunned. He called the waitress over and asked her if she knew who the man was that just left their table? The waitress grinned and said, "Of course. Everybody here knows him. That's Ben Hooper. He's the former governor of Tennessee!" *Dr. Fred Craddock, Seminary professor of homiletics at Emory University in Atlanta.*

By the way—my wife's donation of her pregnant urine for the physiology class I taught my classmates five years before Christopher's birth was never forgotten. I learned my place early in our marriage and kept business at work and home at home. My life has confirmed to me that we are all children of God and I feel that when one celebrates their birthday it's the mother that should be given the recognition and gifts. When Chris celebrates his birthday it's a little more special—he has two mothers.

Shortly after finalizing our adoption of Chris he fell against a wrought iron stair rail and received a black eye. The next weekend at church a friend noticed the eye and commented, "Well I can see your adoption must have been consummated!"

Miss Royal Charm IV

In high school, I took vocational agriculture and was a member of the local FFA organization. I remember Robert's Rules of Order and learning how to conduct a meeting, welding in the machine shop, learning proper animal feeds and feeding practices, attending a National FFA Convention in Kansas City, Kansas, and farm visits. I thought farm visits were the greatest. During these visits, I saw livestock operations that were producing enough income to care for a family. One winter I was not calculating the number of calories needed to maintain my family horses. I felt terrible and embarrassed around my classmates during a visit to my home when our advisor pointed out how thin the horses were getting.

Living on five acres of pasture my options were limited when it came to raising livestock for an FFA project. I purchased a white Milking Shorthorn heifer from my Uncle Bud that stayed at my home or Uncle Bud's ranch from after the fall round-up with Bud's cattle that had been summering on the BLM (Bureau of Land Management) range until in the spring when the cattle were returned to the range. During the time she was staying in my pasture or at my Uncle Bud's ranch, I used her as a hands-on FFA project. Part of her care when she stayed at my home was monitoring her heat cycles and, since there was no bull on the property, at the right time schedule artificial insemination so she would be pregnant (with calf) when returned to the summer range.

My primary FFA project was a New Hampshire pig by the registered papered name of "Miss Royal Charm IV." She was a sweetheart and I could not believe how intelligent she was. Much to the distaste of our neighbors downwind of us with "sensitive noses," my father let me build a pig pen on our property. She raised several litters of pigs there during her time with me. What I noticed is that she would sleep in one part of the pen, eat in another, and another area takes care of her business. She was very clean. My mother would from time-to-time venture into my downstairs bedroom and clean what she called a "Boars Nest." Miss Royal Charm IV was no boar and she also tried not to have a dirty nest. I asked Dana, an employee that has worked at Camden Pet Hospital since it opened in 1969, about a baby pig she found on the side of the road and raised. She let the grown several hundredpound hog into her house. My question to her was, "Did your pet pig make messes in your home?" Her answer was "never!" Something I can't say about any of my pets I let into my house.

The Eastern Idaho State Fair was held in September in my hometown of Blackfoot Idaho. I would coordinate my breeding program with my sow so she would have a litter in time to enter her piglets in the fair. They would be just old enough to be called "weaner pigs" and I would enter them in all the classes available. Most classifications for weaner pigs had none entered but my pigs. So, the judge would guess which small pig would be placed first, second, and so forth, which one would be declared best in class, and best of the breed. I would then place this litter of pigs in their stalls at the fairgrounds with a for sale sign and all the ribbons displayed. The piglets would all be sold at a premium ribbon price and Miss Royal Charm IV and I would go home and prepare for another litter in time for the next state fair.

By the way—Pigs are one of the smartest animals in the animal kingdom. Most ratings of the smartest 15 animals in the world list pigs at number 6 or 7 and dogs at 9 or 10. I've worked mostly with dogs, cats, and rabbits during my professional career as a veterinarian. With the experiences I've had with them and my numerous pets, I can believe these ratings. Dogs are smart, cats set the rules and rabbits don't say much; but, none of them were consciously clean or tried to carry on an almost intelligent grunting conversation like Miss Royal Charm IV (Dana told me her pig communicated much the same way with her). And, that's not all—pigs are a very important part of our human existence and not just for eating. In many respects, pigs are in some really important ways one of "man's best friends." I found in my father's autobiography that a lot of the production of alcohol during the prohibition of 1920 to 1933 was near areas where pigs were grown. The reason— the smell of pigs neutralized the smell of the alcohol being produced, therefore becoming one of the "bootleggers" best friends.

Researchers from the National Institutes of Health in 2015 announced that they'd successfully transplanted hearts from genetically engineered pigs into baboons, potentially paving the way for pig-to-human organ transplants in the future, and pig lungs were developed that could be compatible with the human body. But pigs offer more than just a potential source for organ donation. For over 30 years, scientists have been using pigs in several medical fields. Recently, research developed the ability to re-grow human leg muscles using implants made of pig bladder tissue. Michael Swindle, retired veterinary researcher and author of "Swine in the Laboratory" stated, "It just so happens that, despite our differences, many of the pig's biological systems are very similar to our own. They are what's known as a translational research model, so if (something) works in the pig, then it has a high possibility of working in the human." Because of these similarities, scientists have long used pigs to test interventional catheter devices and methods of cardiovascular surgery, as well as to understand how people develop atherosclerosis and get heart attacks. Tissues derived from pig hearts have been used to replace defective heart valves in humans, lasting upwards of 15 years in the human body. Pigs are omnivores like humans and are used to study digestion, metabolic processes, and oral absorption studies of drugs. Human insulin is very similar to pigs and diabetics who needed daily insulin injections relied on pork insulin until the 1980s. The pig's skin can be used for plastic surgery and wound repair, and their kidneys are similar to ours and used for research.

In 2 Peter 2:22 it reads, "But it is happened unto them according to the true proverb, the dog is turned to his own vomit again; and the sow that was washed to her wallowing in the mire." If one has had the privilege of owning a dog, he/she is well aware of how often a dog vomits its ingesta or brings up the thick viscous secreted material from an empty stomach or hacks up from the respiratory passage ways material known as phlegm. They are also aware of how a "dog is turned to his own vomit" and is usually quick to eat it before the owner can clean up the mess. It is interesting how vomiting can also be a healthy natural process in a dog's life. Kerstin Malm wrote in Applied Animal Behavior, "Regurgitation is the disgorging of partially digested food, often carried out to feed pups and young animals. It seems to be an important step in weaning in some canids and in facilitating the transfer from suckling to eating solid food. In a study, this behavior was seen in 60% of Swedish breeder's mother dogs. Also, some other dogs living in the kennels displayed disgorging behavior. There were no differences between breeds noticed and no environmental influences except the complimentary food, which increased the frequency of regurgitation. This behavior begins when the puppies are about 4 weeks of age and there was a strong connection between regurgitation and begging behavior from the pups." Regurgitation in relation to weaning in the domestic dog: a questionnaire study, *Applied Animal Behavior, vol 43, issue 2, Kerstin Malm May 1995, pages 111-122.*

When Peter wrote in the Bible, "the sow that was washed (is turned) to her wallowing in the mire," it reminds me of my experiences with domestic pigs. I was taught and observed that they needed to be kept from stress and too much activity during hot days and that shade, a cool breeze, water to lay in, and mud would keep production at a high level and helped prevent loss of life from over-heating or drinking. Animals can transfer internal heat to the outside of their body by sweating, taking deep rapid breaths of air into and out of their lungs, panting with shallow rapid breaths of air flowing over their moist tongues, or a combination of these. These three are the most important tools for the maintenance of body temperature and form their inbuilt evaporative cooling system. Dogs do not have sweat glands and primarily use air flowing over their moist tongues hanging out to cool down. Cats take rapid breaths when overheated or stressed.

Due to physiological limitations and their relatively thick subcutaneous fat, pigs are prone to heat stress. Pigs lack functional sweat glands and are almost incapable of panting. To thermoregulate, they rely on wallowing in water or mud to cool the body. Mud is the preferred substrate; after wallowing, the wet mud provides a cooling, and probably protecting, layer on the body. But even in cool weather, pigs still wallow, suggesting that the magic of mud doesn't just lie in thermal regulation. I once had a wild piglet brought in that an employee had found near her home. The pig was dehydrated, depressed, covered with lice, and died even though we tried to help it. Wild pigs are known to use mud baths to scrape off parasites such as ticks and lice; they also rub their scent glands around wallowing areas, possibly as a way of territory marking. *Geofftey Joe, Pigs, 11/12/2020.*

As I understand it, Peter in 2 Peter 2:22 wrote about, "The chains of (bad) habits are generally too small to be felt until they are too strong to be broken" Samuel Johnson. And, in repeating a particular sin (bad habit) we embody the wisdom of Proverbs 26:11, "the fool returns to his folly just as a dog returns to eat his own vomit. Similarly, they are like a pig who can be scrubbed clean, but soon returns to wallow in the muck again." This is a particularly pungent analogy for Peter since pigs and dogs are two of the most intelligent animals on earth, who probably used it because at the time they were two of the most despised and unclean animals in Jewish thinking. These scriptures are very descriptive on how difficult it can be to overcome a destructive habit; but, certainly are not the reasons a dog and pig have what seem to be repulsive habits. They are quite reasonable behaviors for the survival of their species.

One afternoon I was checking in on Miss Royal Charm IV and her piglets. I noticed one in the litter had died. I gently nudged it over a couple of times with my foot, finding it limp and not responsive. Since a mother laying on piglets is a common cause of death, I immediately listed in my mind the diagnosis of the pig's demise. I retrieved a shovel from the shed and spent some time digging a grave in the summer's hardened ground. I then went back to retrieve the supposed victim and conduct my planned burial service. When I got back to the pig-pen I could not find either the carcass or evidence that it had been eaten. Counting the piglets several times I realized that there was not a death but a very deep sleeping pig that fooled me into digging its grave.

A man finds in the productions of nature an inexhaustible stock of material on which he can employ himself, without any temptations to envy or malevolence, and has always a certain prospect of discovering new reasons for adoring the sovereign author of the universe. Samuel Johnson

Off To College

Sheryl Gardner and I became good friends during our junior and senior years attending high school in Blackfoot Idaho. During the spring of 1964, I had applied and been accepted to attend the University of Idaho in a small northern town called Moscow. Her father wanted his daughter to attend a university closer to home and did not want to incur the costs involved, risk of traveling such distances and I suspect they were in hopes that Sheryl and I would not become too good of friends and do stupid things away from his watchful eye.

We had a dilemma and word got out to my aunt Nondus Bithell that we would like to attend college together. She was the local county agent, worked a lot with youth in the 4-H program, and was involved in helping them receive secondary education scholarships. One day Nondus called Sheryl and asked her if she might be interested in home economics as a career. She did not know how to respond until Nondus mentioned that there was a good scholarship available at the U of I in the Home Economics Department. She answered that she hadn't declared a major and would like to investigate this option. Her father was even more thrilled—to him having a daughter with a college scholarship was impressive. So that fall he and Sheryl's mother were concerned enough to drive us to Moscow on a mission to learn more about the great U of I situated just five miles east of Washington State University. It's interesting to me that my matchmaker aunt Nondus also encouraged her brother, my future dad, to get in contact with mom when she attended a summer session at the U of I and dad was teaching in the bacteriology department.

Sheryl enjoyed the music. She played the piano and organ well enough to be asked by her religious congregation to play for them on Sundays, sang in the choir in high school, and was on the marching drill team at the U of I. She was big on, as she would say, "real music." As for me, I was attracted to music that had a western theme, with a story to tell and words I could understand. Since my youth, I've had some impaired hearing, and words mixed with music make it worse. I still have some of the vinyl records she collected of "real music" ("ALL-TIME BROADWAY HIT PARADE", "The 120 greatest songs, Arthur Fiedler and the Boston Pops play hits of the '60s & 70's", "Herb Alpert & the Tijuana Brass" . . .) I wasn't particular about what I listened to as long as it was country music. Jonny Cash was one of my favorites. Sheryl called him, "Johnny Trash."

Another artist that I didn't remember his name sang a catchy toon that I remember to this day. It was "I Won't Go Hunting With You Jake But I'll Go Chasing

Women—"Oh, it's springtime in the mountains and I'm full of mountain dew. Can't even read my catalog like I used to do. I'm a-sittin' in that little shed that's right back of the house. Here comes old Jake with all the hounds but he's gonna hear me shout—Oh, I won't go hunting with you, Jake but I'll go chasing women . . ."

I later found out his name was Stuart Hamblin and noticed he had an interesting story to tell. Back in the '50s, he was a well-known radio host/comedian/ songwriter in Hollywood who was noted for his drinking, womanizing, partying, etc. One of his bigger hits at the time was, you guessed it, "I won't go hunting with you Jake, but I'll go chasing women." One day, along came a young preacher holding a tent revival. Hamblin had him on his radio show presumably to poke fun at him. In order to gather more material for his show, Hamblin showed up at one of the revival meetings. Early in the service, the preacher announced, "There is one man in this audience who is a big fake." There were probably others who thought the same thing, but Hamblin was convinced that he was the one the preacher was talking about but he was having none of that.

Still, the words continued to haunt him until a couple of nights later he showed up drunk at the preacher's hotel door around 2AM demanding that the preacher pray for him! But the preacher refused, saying, "This is between you and God and I'm not going to get in the middle of it." But he did invite Stuart in and they talked until about 5 AM at which point Stuart dropped to his knees and with tears, cried out to God. But that is not the end of the story. Stuart quit drinking, quit chasing women, quit everything that was 'fun'. Soon he began to lose favor with the Hollywood crowd. He was ultimately fired by the radio station when he refused to accept a beer company as a sponsor.

Hard times were upon him. He tried writing a couple of "Christian" songs but the only one that had much success was "This Old House", written for his friend Rosemary Clooney. As he continued to struggle, a longtime friend named John took him aside and told him, "All your troubles started when you 'got religion', was it worth it all?" Stuart answered simply, "Yes." Then his friend asked, "You liked your booze so much, don't you ever miss it?" And his answer was, "No". John then said, "I don't understand how you could give it up so easily." And Stuart's response was, "It's no big secret. All things are possible with God". To this John said, "That's a catchy phrase. You should write a song about it." And as they say, "The rest is history."

The song Stuart wrote was "It Is No Secret. It is no secret what God can do. What He's done for others, He'll do for you. With arms wide open, He'll welcome you. It is no secret, what God can do." By the way . . . the friend was John Wayne. And, the young preacher who refused to pray for Stuart Hamblen? . . . That was Billy Graham . . . And, the song has been sung as hits by Jimmy Dean and Elvis Presley.

Yes Nondus, it was amazing what God could do for mom and dad—Sheryl and me too. But it wouldn't have happened if it weren't for you!

True story . . . recently I was discussing with my staff how my wife hated country-western music I enjoyed hearing while we were attending the University of Idaho in the early '60s. I brought up the name of a song I remembered, "I won't go hunting with you Jake, but I'll go chasing women." No one recognized the song, I looked it up and what a surprise awaited me. Not the best song to remember in my youth, but what a wonderful story about a struggling man that found his way.—*W. Rich Hoge, 06/21/2011.*

"It Is No Secret. It is no secret what God can do. What He's done for others, He'll do for you. With arms wide open, He'll welcome you." Stuart Hamblin

Letter to Uncle Bud
July 31, 1999
Roland Colson Rich
1195 West 600 South
Pingree, ID 83262

Dear Uncle Bud,

I would like to thank you and LaRue for the nice visit and lunch I had with you during my recent visit to Idaho. Just seeing the ranch and your home brings back memories of my childhood that are as vivid as if they were yesterday. Mother has always instilled in her children a love for the ranch and we've always felt a part of it.

I will always remember staying at the ranch and sleeping on the porch bundled under several layers of blankets that Grandma Leva Rich had placed over me. Those nights seemed to last forever. My mind would be filled with the excitement of the coming day's activities of getting up before daybreak, starting a fire in the old cast iron stove, herding in the cows to milk, milking, bringing the milk cans to the house, and placing wet burlap bags around them to keep them cool, shooting a white duck I should not have with my BB gun, having a "real" breakfast and the chance to go to the blue hole and fish.

You would place the cows in their stalls, hobble them, give me a one-legged stool and a bucket, point out a cow and tell me to fill the bucket with milk. The cow's teats were swollen and hard making it almost impossible for my small hands to produce milk. After a couple of minutes, the cow seemed to either blow her nose or wet on me. Then I would notice that Uncle Bud smile as you shot another squirt of warm wet milk my way. I've always loved the smell of cows and what goes with them. It's probably because of my early experiences at the ranch.

I used to spend hours fishing the creek and blue hole at the ranch. Occasionally I would catch a fish, but it was usually a whitefish or sucker. But when you took me fishing it was the best. I remember sitting on a gravel bar on the Snake River in the dark being eaten to death by mosquitoes while fishing with minnows. You were upstream and had told me where to cast the bait and how to bring the line in. I was cold, wet, had mosquito bites all over my body, and was wishing for the words "Rich, the moon was out last night and the fish must not be hungry, Let's go home." When suddenly my pole was nearly pulled out of my hands. The adrenaline rushed through my body as I waited for the next strike. It happened, I pulled back on the line and the fun began but only for a few short seconds. The fishing line again fell limp and the fish was gone. The call soon came for us to go home. Not only was I cold, wet, and mosquito-bitten but I also got to hear from you as to how to properly set a hook and how that fish was probably the great giant grandpa fish you had been trying to catch for years.

A real highlight for me was when I went with you as the cattle were being taken to the summer range. I got to ride in the cattle truck alone with you and you gave me your full attention. I remember you really impressed me when you peeled a grapefruit and ate it. At the time I thought it was the biggest orange I had ever seen. When I grew-up I wanted to eat big oranges just like you. Ear tagging, branding, and vaccinating the calves were just the greatest. This experience helped gel my interest in agriculture and later in life, I joined FFA in high school and bought that white Milking Short Horn heifer from you as a project. You would take her to the summer range (or she was bred by artificial insemination when at my home) for breeding and then in the fall bring her back to your ranch or my house. She fell on the ice one winter and never recovered. I took her to the slaughterhouse and she had abscesses throughout her body. I wondered why and thoughts began running through my mind about veterinary medicine.

I remember your brothers and sisters did things together. You had a large garden behind the sheds with, as I remember, rows of beans, peas, corn, and squash. Everyone would get together to harvest and bottle the vegetables. It seemed to take forever to snap beans. One summer I picked a handful of peas and ate them. I had an allergic reaction that gave me a good scare.

Slaughtering chickens was most impressive. As I recall, you would catch them using a stick with a loop of wire on the end, tie the chicken's legs together, hang them upside down and make a cut in the roof of their mouth. The chickens would hang there and slowly bleed to death cackling away without showing any signs of suffering. That seemed much better than having the head cut off and flopping all over the place.

Part of our visit to the ranch included a trip to the spring and harvesting some watercress when it was in season. I never could figure out why that pipe, down the hill from the ranch house, with water coming out of it never ran out of water. All I knew is that the water was cold and tasted good. The only downside was the snakes encountered going to and from the pipe.

Thank you for helping me by being a role model for me during my early life. Whether it is my last memory of Grandpa Chase Rich closing the gate as we were leaving the ranch, you shooting at high flying geese off your porch with a 30 06 rifle, the pictures of you and your dad fishing or hunting placed on the family room old wood stove, you playing baseball with your grand and great-grandchildren or me being treated special by my Uncle Bud—it was all great.

Sincerely,
Rich Hoge

Pets, Where We Go, and Us Disney Land 1967

Part of my honeymoon over twenty-seven (written 1994) years ago was a trip to Disney Land. For several years my wife's family had made this attraction a part of their Christmas vacation and it was obvious she was convinced Disney Land was truly the "Happiest Place on Earth" (as posted on the park entrance billboard). On the other hand, I was a twenty-one-year-old guy that had never been to the park and must have been too old to have a positive bonding experience. I found the park crowded, long lines at the rides, not enough places to sit down, and the hot pavement and smog too much. I couldn't understand why people would take time from their busy lives to spend their hard-earned money in such an environment. I must admit after having five children I appreciate Disney Land and see more clearly why people enjoy being there.

When you look at owning a pet from a purely practical view—isn't its possession somewhat like visiting Disney Land? Who in their right mind would have such a thing that places so many stresses on our personal lives? They are no more than a liability with constant demands on our time and resources. We must feed, clean up after, exercise, train, find a place for when gone, get groomed, and take places most of us would rather not go (like a veterinarian's office). How many times have I heard a client say, "when she/he's gone there will be no more pets?" However, in a short time after she/he is really gone, they are back in with a new companion. They have been bonded with their previous pet and realize that even with all the effort having a non-human companion is one of the most fulfilling experiences one can have while living on this earth.

I feel there is much that can be learned from Disney Land. This company has captured the vision of helping people truly enjoy life whether in the rain, shoulder to shoulder people, or tagging along with five children for twelve hours. If the experience of owning a pet is somewhat like visiting Disney Land maybe we can apply some of the Disney Company's successes in our family life:

Employees are made to feel special at Disney Land. They are not employees. They are members of the cast. Their clothes are not uniforms—they are costumes. At Disneyland, the employees come to work on buses that have painted on their sides "CAST VIP." The employees are ever-present with a smile on their faces and guess what—no one has ever told me what I couldn't do or it was company policy etc. They were polite and eager to tell me what I could do by saying, "may I help you". When introducing an attraction they would state "Disney Company, Coca Cola,

Delta Airlines, etc and I welcome you and hope you enjoy the . . ." There was always the "I" mentioned—helping them feel that they were an important part of the organization (which they are the most important part). Employees always seem to get along well with each other. I stood out of view watching an employee trying to train a "greenie." She was having trouble getting him to understand and I could tell she was frustrated; but, she never lost her cool or was impolite.

In the hotel there are constant reminders of how happy you are to be in Disney Land. A sign on the path leading to the hotel states "HAVE A GOOD DAY." At the reception desk if a cashier space is vacant they place a nice potted plant in the opening rather than a sign saying "closed or use the next window." At checkout time there is an envelope waiting on the outside doorknob of your room with a note thanking you for staying in the park. Each morning there also is a newspaper outside your door (even on the day you are to check out). In the hotel the complimentary soap and shampoo containers have such positive messages as "IT FEELS SO GOOD TO BE CLEAN", "I'M GOING TO HAVE A WONDERFUL DAY", AND "EVERYBODY NEAT AND PRETTY? THEN ON WITH THE SHOW." Even where there is wet paint the signs used are of Donald Duck busy making a mess with a paintbrush stating that there was wet paint in the area (who could be upset with not being able to use an area of the hotel with this approach?).

Disney Land is always clean. Hours are spent during the night cleaning the park and the area is patrolled by cast members assigned to an area during the day. There is music appropriate for each attraction to help make the lines seem shorter and trees and shrubbery help keep one cool. Where an attraction is not currently in use there are signs with a picture of Mickey Mouse in a hard hat with plans under his arm stating, "PLEASE PARDON OUR APPEARANCE. THIS AREA IS CURRENTLY BEING REFURBISHED FOR YOUR FUTURE ENJOYMENT." The shops are neat, clean, and kept a comfortable temperature. Even though I am sure there is theft in the park, you don't see armed guards standing at the doors. The atmosphere is upbeat and there are appropriately dressed cast members for each store's theme. I noticed when a cash register is closed there is no comment of "CLOSED". The sign reads, "WE'RE SURE SORRY WE MISSED YOU. PLEASE COME BACK AND LET US BE OF SERVICE TOO!". Also, to make things as comfortable as possible, the stores will arrange packages to be delivered to the main gate for later pick up (also makes it a little easier to spend more money).

Probably the most distasteful activity in any theme park with children is eating. You have spent big bucks getting into the park ($36.00 currently in Disney Land) and stretched the pocketbook even more by visiting the shops. Now the family wants to eat and it isn't cheap. Disney has helped make this a less painful experience by enforcing the theme of the "HAPPIEST PLACE ON EARTH." They have placed adds on the throwaway food containers used in the park. The napkins, dishes, plates, and "food serving boxes" have statements such as: "OH BOY! MEALTIME! WHAT DO I WANT . . .", "GOLLY THIS FOOD SURE LOOKS GOOD!", "WOW"! THIS PLACE IS THE BEST SURPRISE I'VE SEEN TODAY", THIS IS A GREAT PLACE TO HAVE FUN!", "WOW THERE IS SO MUCH TO DO HERE!", "BOY, THIS SURE LOOKS GOOD!", "WOW THERE IS SO MUCH TO DO! WHAT SHOULD I SEE NEXT . . .", "I'M THIRSTY! WHAT DO I WANT TO DRINK . . ." I was so impressed by the character designs and messages that I have a collection of "throw-aways" in my motivational materials drawer. *Walter R. Hoge, comments on pets and amusement parks 1994.*

It's interesting how two people can approach similar circumstances with entirely different outlooks. The optimist tries to look on the bright side, believes that good days are ahead, and holds on to the hope that things will get better. The pessimist sees dark rain clouds even on sunny days and believes that the best has passed him by. There's no question whom we'd rather be around. As one commentator writes: "Optimists . . . make life better just by being part of it. They enjoy people, places, and things. Their enthusiasm is contagious. . . The greatest gift anyone can give another is a positive attitude, a smile, and genuine interest. Some claim the only person you can change is yourself. Not true! You can and do change everyone with whom you come in contact. The question is whether you add to or subtract from the day's experience. When our companion pet greets us at the door, when we have an enjoyable uplifting experience visiting places away from home, or a smile and an optimistic I appreciate you hug awaiting even when you have had a "not so good a day"—it makes it easier to have a happier more optimistic assurance that good days will come our way again. Some people seem to have more hopeful dispositions, more natural cheerfulness, and more affirmative expectations. But most of us are not always the optimist or always the pessimist. There's probably a little bit of both in all of us. We'd like to be the optimist more often, but depending on the day, the weather, the aches, and pains, the disappointments and challenges we face, that can be harder than it sounds. Even during our difficult moments, however, we can decide to be happier, more positive today than we may have been yesterday. Optimism is learned; we can practice and work at it until it becomes a habit. We can talk to ourselves and others in more upbeat ways, look for the bright side, and resolve to be more optimistic. When we do, our optimism is a gift not only to ourselves but to everyone around us. *Music and the Spoken Word, Optimism, July 11, 2010.*

"May our lives find us each and every day enjoying a special "Happiest Place on Earth"

Good Intentions Going
Bad May Not Be So Bad

The summer of 1972 between my junior and senior years in veterinary school at Purdue University I was awarded a Mead-Johnson Fellowship studying collie dogs with an inheritable genetic defect called Gray Collie Syndrome. It is characterized by a drastic decline in the number of white blood cells produced in their bodies. This usually occurs every 10 to 12 days, after which the cells rebound. With the important role of white blood cells in the immune system, this sudden drop has a severe negative impact on the dog's overall health. The white blood cells recover and the cycle repeats itself. Affected pups appear to be weaker and can be recognized by their greyer or lighter colored fur in any color compared to the fur of the other healthy pups. The infected are continuously ill and their life expectancy is usually less than three years.

In our studies, we were trying to determine if the thyroid gland was involved in Gray Collie Syndrome and if thyroid hormone levels in the body fluctuated as the white blood cells did. Thyroid hormone controls metabolism in the body and is the one often claimed to be low (hypothyroidism) by women having a hard time controlling their body weight. We found that there were no differences between Gray Collie Syndrome puppies and their littermates. Therefore, we eliminated thyroid hormone as being part of the syndrome but did not shed any new light on the disease. These results were of some value; however, the researcher is always looking for success in gaining an understanding of how Mother Nature works by validating his/her proposed hypothesis. Second-guessing and making decisions without careful observations and study can result in unintended consequences.

One day, a small opening appeared in a cocoon; a man sat and watched the butterfly for several hours as it struggled to force its body through that little hole. Then, it seemed to stop making any progress and appeared to have gotten as far as it could and it couldn't go any farther. So, the man decided to help the butterfly: he took a pair of scissors and opened the cocoon. The butterfly then emerged easily. But its body was withered, it was tiny and had shriveled wings. The man continued to watch because he expected that, at any moment, the wings would open, enlarge and expand, to be able to support the butterfly's body, and become firm. Neither happened! The butterfly spent the rest of its life crawling around with a withered body and shriveled wings. It never was able to fly.

What the man, in his kindness and his goodwill did not understand was that the restricting cocoon and the struggle required for the butterfly to get through the tiny opening, were nature's way of forcing fluid from the body of the butterfly into its wings, so that it would be ready for flight once it achieved its freedom from the cocoon. Sometimes, struggles are exactly what we need in our life. If we were allowed to go through life without any obstacles, it would cripple us. We would not be as strong as we could have been. We would have never been able to fly. "Difficulty is a severe instructor, set over us by the supreme guardian and legislator, who knows us better than we know ourselves and loves us better too. He that wrestles with us strengthens our nerves and sharpens our skill. Our antagonist is our helper." *Edmund Burke.*

Carefully evaluating the data and our disappointments working with the Gray Collie Syndrome puppies resulted in discovering important information about thyroid hormone. The procedure we were using to evaluate the presence of the hormone involved the use of thyroid-stimulating hormone (TSH) that is produced by the pituitary gland located at the base of the brain. This is the primary hormone that stimulates the thyroid gland to produce thyroid hormone. We would inject this TSH into the experimental dogs and collect blood samples before the injection and at 1, 4, 8, 12, and 24 hours after the injection. What we found was that TSH elevated the thyroid hormone levels in the Gray Collie Syndrome dogs by more than three times (7 ug) their normal levels (1.7 ug). These elevated values peeked in 8 to 12 hours. We then did the same tests on normal dogs and found the same results; but, the hypothyroid dogs' thyroid level (0.8 ug) did not change when given TSH injections. As I remember, up until this time veterinarians felt that the thyroid hormone would peak at 24 hours because that was what happened when humans were given the TSH test. When we were using the thyroid values at 24 hours (5 ug) it was less obvious how much the dog had responded to the TSH. Because of this study veterinarians began using the 8 to 12-hour blood values to be more accurate in diagnosing hypothyroidism. *Response To Thyrotropin as a Diagnostic Aid for Canine Hypothyroidism, W. R. Hoge, et al, Journal of the American Animal Hospital, Vol 10, No 2 March/April 1974.*

A.B. Bragdon stated, "Alas, how scant the sheaves for all the trouble, the toil, the pain and the resolve sublime.—a few full ears; the rest but weeds and stubble, and withered wildflowers plucked before their time." Let this be a lesson to all of us during our lives. "Ask, and it shall be given you; seek, and you will find; knock, and it shall be opened unto you" Mathew 7:7. It may not be what we are asking, seeking, or knocking for but when we find it—it will probably be better than we ever expected.

For the scant results, we found from all our troubles, the toil and reams of useless data we produced, the painful realization that we were not successful in our hypothesis, and all we thought we found was as worthless as weeds, stubble, and withered flowers—we found but one full ear of success and that contributed to the advancement of helping care for our canine patients with hypothyroidism . . .

Chico the Wallaby and
the Other Guy

During my senior year at veterinary school, a brown-colored short-haired dachshund dog was hospitalized to be euthanized because of a broken back leg, and the owner having insufficient funds to have the fractured bone repaired. I was at that time assigned to the small animal clinic and noticed the red euthanasia sticker on a cage door with the name Bernie. After investigating the case I asked the head of surgery if I could repair the leg. He told me that the hospital must provide the service a client requested. However, if I wanted to call the client and get his permission my surgical team could do the surgery. I called the client and was told, "If that (blankety-blank) dog leaves the state of Indiana you have my permission to repair the leg. I placed a stainless-steel pin in Bernie's leg, it healed as hoped and I found myself owning my first dog.

Not long after taking him to my apartment, I became fully aware of why the owner used unprintable words to describe Bernie. There was an alleyway behind my

61

apartment and during an attempt to take Bernie for a walk around half a block, he just sat there when I pulled on his leash. Finally, in frustration, I dropped the leash went for my walk alone and upon returning Bernie wagged his tail, looked at me as if asking, "Have you had a wonderful walk?" and headed for the door. This was the true Bernie. During his life living as a part of my family he was stubborn, had "a my way or the highway attitude", didn't get along with my wife or children kind of a guy. It didn't take long before I knew why the owner wanted Bernie dead or out of the state of Indiana. Several times my wife asked me if I would put Bernie to sleep (euthanize). I finally told her, "I'll put the needle in if you will push the plunger." It never happened. Though Bernie became blind he lived a long life. Unfortunately, while we were on vacation a storm blew down our fence next to our neighbor's swimming pool and he drowned.

Several years into veterinary practice I cared for two well-trained chestnut-colored long-haired dachshunds with wonderful temperaments living in what appeared to be a loving home. One day I received a call from the owner telling me that she had just purchased a male wallaby in Nevada (they are not legal in California), bought a manual on caring for such an animal, and wanted me to care for her new friend who she called Chico. She dropped off the thick complete manual on how to take care of the members of the animal family called Macropodidae—meaning bigfoot. Over a year or two I didn't see much of Chico until one day the owner called me and said that I needed to put Chico down. Apparently, her husband was taking Chico to his pen and Chico put his mouth into her husband's crotch and bit "very hard." Evidently Chico felt the husband was a territorial threat to his relationship with his wife. I understand that wallabies don't normally bite. This is the behavior I've seen from fights between tom cats. I once had a young tom presented with his jewels hanging out of the scrotal sac who evidently could not run fast enough out of another's territory.

Wallabies look like kangaroos, they stand on their back legs and eat with their front paws. They are stocky and powerful with shaggy fur and bare black snouts. Males can weigh up to 100 pounds, while females rarely get larger than 50 pounds. Pet wallabies are rare in the United States as most states ban their ownership. Wallabies are shy, and it takes time to teach them to socialize. However, they are curious and will bond quite nicely with their owners if well-raised (while still nursing), socialized, and treated positively. They don't mix well with other animals and can be friendly, playful, and affectionate, but also mischievous, albeit entertaining. Wallabies can understand "no," but they need firm corrections and never physical punishment. Wallabies are herbivores, naturally grazing on grasses and shrubs in their natural environment. In captivity, they need to be given a constant supply of fresh, good-quality hay (such as Bermuda, alfalfa, or ryegrass). *Wallabies: Species Profile, Characteristics, Housing, Diet, and Other Information, Lianne McLeod, DVM, Updated 06/07/20.* In a study by June E. Olds, the aggressiveness between male wallabies in captivity is problematic enough that Prozac (a medication used for several mental issues in humans) has been studied to help keep the peace. I suspect this was Chico's problem with his owner's husband. *Use Of Oral Fluoxetine For The Treatment Of Abnormal Aggression In Two Red-Necked Wallabies, June E. Olds, J. of Zoo and Wildlife Medicine, 48(3):922-924, 2017.*

The relationship between human male anger and violence is even more complex than wallabies and cats. What's not nearly as complicated is the relationship between human masculinity and anger and aggression.

Here are five things we know:

1. Masculinity is associated with anger: In a 2014 study from the University of South Australia, Michelle Wharton and colleagues found through questionnaires that masculine participants reported greater anger than feminine participants and not simply that males were angrier than females. In fact, females who had a more masculine gender identity were angrier than females with more feminine gender identity.

2. When men's masculinity is threatened, they react with increased anger: in a 2015 study by Julia Dahl and colleagues from Penn State University found that when masculinity was challenged, men reacted with more anger and with an increased endorsement of social dominance over women.

3. Challenging men's testosterone levels yields a similar effect: Similar findings come from a 2016 study from the University of Gdansk, where Kosakowska-Berezecka

and colleagues found that telling men they have low levels of testosterone served as a threat to masculinity and led to engagement in more "gender-stereotypical behaviors," like getting into physical fights. Meanwhile, men who were told they had high testosterone levels were more likely to support gender equality and more likely to engage in stereotypically feminine behaviors, like caretaking or doing housework.

4. Masculinity is also related to right-wing authoritarian attitudes: According to a 2014 study from Bradley Goodnight and colleagues at Georgia State University, there are three dimensions, in particular, that related to masculinity: status (a belief that men should be respected and project an air of confidence), toughness (a belief that men should be physically tough and aggressive), and antifemininity (a belief that men should avoid stereotypically feminine activities).

5. "Dormant masculinity" becomes visible when men get drunk: a 2015 study from Rushelle Leone randomly assigned students to consume alcoholic or non-alcoholic beverages before completing an aggression paradigm in which they administered or received electric shocks to/from a fictitious opponent. Participants who valued toughness and had anti-feminine attitudes were more aggressive toward their opponent when they were (a) intoxicated and (b) believed their opponent was gay because of information they had received about him earlier. The authors describe this as "dormant masculinity." *Psychology Today, Ryan Martin, Ph.D.*

So, what about Chico? I don't believe that right-wing authoritarian or drunken attitudes are attributed to his behavior. However, I can certainly believe testosterone levels, inter-male mating aggression, and real or imagined threats could be the answer. I called the vocational agriculture (FFA) instructor at Pioneer High School, with whom I was helping out in his classroom, to see if there was an answer for Chico. His class cared for some exotics, such as endangered desert turtles, that he had a State of California permit to care for. He made a few calls, he could get a permit for Chico, we planned on Chico staying at Camden Pet Hospital where he would be neutered (removal of those jewels) and when socialized for a few weeks become a ward of Pioneer High School. The surgery went fine, Chico was found to be a very shy nervous guy, adjusted ok in the hospital, and showed no aggression. After a few years living at Pioneer High School, he was retired to a kangaroo ranch in northern California and lived out his life with his kind.

I was involved with youth in the scouting program for many years. Several of the scouts stilled lived in the area when they married. Before the wedding, I would sit down with them and give them some fatherly advice and gave them a gift. I started by showing them a beautiful soft leather money pouch made from a kangaroo's scrotum. Then I would show them a new shiny Susan B. Anthony dollar coin. I placed it into the pouch and told them as the years go by, just as time in contact with tannic acid from in this pouch, his new bride will tarnish and not look as she does today. Then I told them that if they decided to get a new model wife, as I placed another new coin in the pouch, that wife would also tarnish as she got older. Then not only would they have one tarnished wife but two and both of them would have control of him for the rest of his life. Last year one of these boys' mom passed and while the divorced and remarried son was in town for the funeral, he called and asked me to give this presentation to his son. And I did.

The laws of nature are just, but terrible. There is no weak mercy in them. Cause and consequence are inseparable and inevitable. The elements have no forbearance. The fire burns, the water drowns, the air consumes, the earth buries. And perhaps it would be well for our race if the punishment of crimes against the laws of man were as inevitable as the punishment of crimes against the laws of nature,— were man as unerring in his judgments as nature. Henry Wadsworth Longfellow

During a routine visit with the previous owner of Chico and the two long-haired dachshunds she made the statement, "Doctor Hoge, you neutered the wrong guy—it should have been my husband." She then informed me that she had recently divorced.

For as the churning of milk produces butter, and wringing the nose produces blood, so the forcing of wrath produces strife. Proverbs 30:33

Thoughts About My Mother
The Eager Beaver

Beavers are among the largest living rodents in the world. They have thick fur, webbed feet, and flattened scale-covered tails. With powerful jaws and strong teeth, they fell trees to build lodges (homes) and dams, often changing their environment in ways few other animals can. They live in or around freshwater ponds, lakes, rivers, marshes, and swamps. Beavers are primarily nocturnal. They spend most of their time eating and building lodges. Beavers build dams to make ponds by weaving branches together, felling trees by cutting them down with their teeth and waterproofing the dam and lodges with mud.

The beaver is a keystone species, increasing biodiversity in its territory through the creation of ponds and wetlands. As wetlands are formed and riparian habitats are enlarged, aquatic plants colonize newly available watery habitats. Insect, invertebrates, fish, mammals, and bird diversities are also expanded. Beaver ponds increase stream flows in seasonally dry streams by storing run-off in the rainy season, which raises groundwater tables via percolation from beaver ponds. Beaver ponds have been shown to remove sediment thus improving stream water quality. In addition, fecal bacteria excreted into streams by grazing cattle are reduced by slowing currents that settle the bacteria to the bottom. Beavers help waterfowl by creating increased areas of water, they thaw areas of open water, allowing an earlier nesting season and increase bat populations. Beaver ponds have been shown to have a beneficial effect on trout and salmon populations. The fish are also larger, more numbers of small fish survive living in beaver ponds, grow faster, and are in better condition. The surface of beaver ponds is typically at or near bankfull, so even small increases in streamflow cause the pond to overflow its banks and spread water and nutrients beyond the stream banks. Finally, beaver ponds may serve as critical firebreaks in fire-prone areas.

Oregon is called "The Beaver State" because of the association of beavers with the early history of the state and because of the admirable qualities of intelligence, industry, and ingenuity that are associated with this animal. Merriam Webster defines an eager beaver as, "A person who is extremely zealous about performing duties and volunteering for more." Throughout my life, my mother lived as the dictionary and Beaver State defines this animal.

When Mother's Day approaches, I am often reminded of one of the last acts of Eager Beaver Hood she extended to me.

One of the events I have stored in my imaginary scrape book of my mother's life is a telephone conversation I had with her. She was in her eighties and at her home one cold day in Idaho with snow on the ground and ice on the roads. I was comfortably sitting in a chair on a bright sunny winter day in my California home. I casually mentioned that I needed a copy of my Social Security card and wondered if she still had one at her home. I wasn't worried about it because I knew that I could get one online and have a new card issued if I couldn't find mine. The next day Mother called and told me that she had found my Social Security card, drove on icy roads in the dark, waited until the post office opened and my card was sent overnight delivery to me. And, "please let her know when it arrives."

Talk about a guilt trip—my arthritic, hard of hearing and doesn't see the best mother going out of her way on a dark cold morning, scrapped the ice off her car's windshield, and drove on slick icy roads to help a lazy fifty-something-year-old son that hadn't even made an effort to look carefully in his safe for his Social Security card. I could only imagine the obituary page in the newspaper: "Mrs. Hoge passed away shortly after sliding off an icy road in the early morning light on her way to the post office to send an important letter to her eldest son, Rich."

Like a dog has anal glands that need to be cleaned at times, both the male and female beavers also have anal glands but in addition, there is a caster gland, which is located a short gasp away from its anal gland, right under its big tail. Technically called castoreum, there's a musk-like substance produced described as "brown slime" that is used to mark territory. A beaver's posterior, believe it or not, smells good.

Like, really good, according to Joanne Crawford, a wildlife ecologist who told National Geographic that she loves putting her nose down there and breathing it all in. "People think I'm nuts," she said. "I tell them, 'Oh, but it's beavers; it smells really good.'" Castoreum is so favorably fragrant that we've been using it to flavor ice cream, chewing gum, pudding, and brownies—basically, anything that could use vanilla, raspberry, or strawberry substitute—for at least 80 years. It also has been used in perfume, cigarettes, Sweden to produce schnapps, and medically it has been used for anxiety, insomnia, menstrual cramps, and other conditions, but there isn't enough scientific evidence to support these uses. Is Beaver Butt Really Used To Flavor Your Dessert? Here's What You Should Know, Castoreum has been used for centuries, By James Cave 12/11/2020 + other sources.

An old Jewish saying states that "God could not be everywhere, and therefore he made mothers." Mothers everywhere do His work on earth. This divine work includes the demanding but rewarding sacrifices of child-rearing. Mothers teach and inspire, comfort and encourage, and even take time out for fun. And a mother is a mother all her life and I'll bet into the eternities. I was super lucky in having an extra special Eager Beaver Hood Mom who kept ice off the pond, a warm protected lodge full of good smells with plenty of food stored away, and caring love for the good and bad times.

Every Life is a Wonderful Story

When Bocelli was born (09/22/1958) doctors had advised the couple to abort him, as they predicted that the child would be born with a disability. It was evident at birth that Bocelli had numerous problems with his sight, and he was eventually diagnosed with congenital glaucoma. Bocelli showed a great passion for music as a young boy. His nanny Oriana gave him the first record of Franco Corelli, and he began to show interest in pursuing the career of a tenor. By age 7, he was able to recognize the famous voices of the time and tried to emulate the great singers. At age 12. Bocelli lost his sight completely following an accident during a soccer game. He was hit in the eye playing goalkeeper during a match and suffered a brain hemorrhage. Doctors resorted to leeches in a last-ditch effort to save his sight, but they were unsuccessful and he remained blind.

In the movie "The Music of Silence," Bocelli tells his own story in the form of an autobiographical novel, naming his alter Amos Bardi. He writes of a loving family that encouraged his musical gifts from an early age and of the dedication that led to his professional breakthrough and his meteoric rise to stardom. The accomplishments Andrea has made in his life have not been easy on him or his family. In most cases, greatness comes from attitude and a lot of effort. Jeffrey R. Holland has commented, "If for a while the harder you try, the harder it gets, take heart. So, it has been with the best people who ever lived." *The Inconvenient Messiah, BYU Speeches, Feb 15, 1982.*

David O. McKay brings to light the quote that life begins and ends with family in the statement, "The home is the first and most effective place to learn the lessons of life: truth, honor, virtue, self-control, the value of education, honest work, and the purpose and privilege of life. Nothing can take the place of home in rearing and teaching children, and no other success can compensate for failure in the home."

Also, nothing can be more critical than family in the animal kingdom. They have an inborn spirit of responsibility of who they are and their role in raising a family. I enjoy watching the geese in Boise Idaho's public park during the spring and early summer. There are what seems like hundreds of goslings in the lake and on its shoreline all being kept close and in sight by a few adult geese. They are taking turns as babysitters and giving a chance for the parents of these goslings to get some food and a little rest and relaxation.

This is not unusual behavior amongst animals. Elephants are called "all mothers" helping ensure the newborns' survival, Orangutan mothers maintain physical contact with their babies for the entire first four months of its life and the female alligator guards her nest until her litter is born and then spends the next year protecting her babies from predators with a lot of the time being spent keeping her babies safe inside her mouth. Female octopuses separate her thousands of laid eggs into those most likely to survive, she then dedicates the next two months protecting them from predators and ensuring they get enough oxygen pushes water currents towards the eggs. Because she is so busy keeping them alive, she doesn't have time to feed herself—so she often ends up passing away shortly after they hatch. After giving birth the female Emperor penguin leaves the family behind to replenish her body at sea, leaving the father to take on all of the parental responsibilities. For two months, the father will carry his egg around on his feet and forgo eating until the mother returns. When she does, she'll regurgitate some of her food for the newly hatched baby, while the father takes his turn out at sea.

Watching over the family is not only seen in wild animals. There are numerous examples of domesticated animals looking out for their kind as well as others—even humans. Sandy Adams a client of mine sent me this letter I had requested from her. "I have been very fortunate to have been owned by many memorable Yorkies, but there was one that never demanded much, preferring to stay in the background and follow me wherever I went. We came to call this lovely little guy 'our Caretaker' although his call name was 'Bully'. We also shared our home with a Yorkie we called Peaches. Peach was a happy, outgoing, feisty little girl . . . in other words a typical Yorkie! When she was diagnosed diabetic, we were devastated as we were certain she would not live much longer; however, Dr. Hoge assured us otherwise and, with care, she lived many more happy years . . . blind.

Animals, as we all know, are simply amazing. When Peaches became blind we worried she would never find her way in and out of the doggie door, navigate our large yard, etc. But we had a secret weapon—our lovely Caretaker! He immediately assessed the situation, went over to Peaches, put his rear under her chin, and led her to the doggie door, out and around our upper yard. Once she realized she could find her way, she just took off . . . literally! It was fascinating to watch our girl as she did not appear blind to anyone who did not know. Obstacles were simply no problem, she would run and play seeming to sense anything in her way, lightly flipping her paws slightly in front of her. But Bully . . . well, he never quit watching over her. He would stand at the French doors and watch her, following her out should she get out of his sight.

Our little caretaker was special in yet another way . . . he was the last of our lineage. When he was fourteen, we introduced him to our new puppy. He immediately checked her out, washed her a bit, and let her chew contentedly on his ears. Afraid of the doggie door, she refused to go out on her own. Bully came to the rescue; he promptly opened the doggie door, stood in it to hold it open so she could go out between his little legs! He watched his new charge until the day he left us.

No one can ever tell me these pets cannot reason—this story, as well as many others, have proven they are more than just remarkable creatures." *(Sandy Adams, client and friend of Camden Pet Hospital, "The Caretaker and the Peach", Feb 24, 2015).*

"The family is one of nature's masterpieces." George Santayana "They are the compass that guides us. They are the inspiration to reach great heights and our comfort when we occasionally falter." Brad Henry

> *"Dear Veronica (Bocelli's wife), my dear children, every life is a wonderful story worthy of being told. Every life is a work of art, and if it does not seem so, perhaps it is only necessary to illuminate the room that contains it.*
>
> *The secret is never to lose faith, to have confidence in God's plan for us, revealed in the signs with which He shows us the way. If you learn to listen, you will find that each life speaks to us of love. Because love is the key to everything, the engine of the world. Love is the secret energy behind every note I sing. And never forget that there's no such thing as happenstance. That's an illusion lawless and arrogant men invented so that they could sacrifice the truth of our world to the laws of reason.*
>
> *Andrea Bocelli—stated during credits given for the movie "The Music Of Silence."*

Curse and Hate Letters

Citizens of the Roman Empire had a habit of writing when they were wronged. They etched grievances into thin sheets of lead, which were rolled and pierced with nails, then buried in tombs or thrown into wells. There was no gripe too small. Researchers have found more than 1,500 curse tables, including 130 around Aquae Sulis (now Bath, England) seeking revenge for shoes and other items stolen while their owners were in the water. Some are signs; some depict the perpetrator. Many petitions a deity with powers to befoul the suspect's life. Why do such complaints matter? They're documents of the common people's concerns, "says *Celia Sanchez Natalias of Spain's University of Zaragoza,*" not Augustus's or Cicero's. A newly translated 1,600-year-old tablet contained two interesting curses. One of the curses targets a Roman senator named Fistus and appears to be the only known example of a cursed senator. The other curse targets a veterinarian (now we're getting too close for my comfort) named Porcello. Ironically, Porcello is the Latin word for pig.

Celia Sanchez Natalias, a doctoral student at the University of Zaragoza, explained that Porcello was probably his name. "In the world of curse tablets, one of the things that you have to do is to try to identify your victim in a very, very, exact way." She added that it isn't certain who cursed Porcello or why. It could be for either personal or professional reasons. "Maybe this person was someone that (had) a horse or an animal killed by Porcello's medicine. Destroy, crush, kill, strangle, Porcello, and wife Maurilla. Their soul, heart, buttocks, liver . . ." part of it reads. The iconography on the tablet shows a mummified Porcello, his arms crossed (as is the deity), and his name written on both arms. *Black Magic Revealed in Two Ancient Curses, Owen Jarus, LiveScience Contributor, May 22, 2012.*

Like the citizens of Rome (as well as other ancient civilizations) many of us have written hate tablets that were never sent. This includes well-known individuals such as Abraham Lincoln, Harry S. Truman, Winston Churchill, and Mark Twain. Their written letters of anger (curse tablets) have been found filed away and never sent. *(Sunday Review, NY Times, Marie Konnikova March 22, 2014).* Why weren't they torn up and thrown away or burned? I suspect that deep down inside these folks hoped that the letters would somehow find their addressee when they would not have to face them.

In a lot of ways, probably little has changed over the years in the art of unsent curse letters. We may have switched the format from paper to screen, but the process is largely the same. You feel angry or hurt. And you construct a retort—only to find yourself thinking better of taking it any further. Emotions cooled, you proceed in a more reasonable, and reasoned, fashion. The "curse tablet" becomes a problem when you write the comments in a text, on Facebook, Tweet, etcetera, and push the send button before the emotions have cooled.

At my work we "fire" clients that are difficult to work with and express some of the feelings noted in the 1600-year-old hate tablet written for the poor Roman shamed veterinarian. On one occasion a client wanted to visit in person the female veterinarian on our staff that requested he be fired from future services. The veterinarian involved was very anxious and concerned about what the man may say or do when she was in the room alone with him. I told her that I would be right outside of the exam room during her visit and if the situation got out of control I would open the door and intervene. Thankfully, the man presented himself on bended knee apologizing for his actions and explaining his difficult situations at home. He expressed the desire to continue bringing his pet to our hospital and we had a very good working relationship with the family from then on.

I've found over the years that people, in general, are easy to get along with. Usually, if there are problems in a relationship it is because I have not communicated well with the client or there are pressing issues and stresses in an individual's personal life that leads them to lash out. According to Sandy Walsh an instructor for Patterson Veterinary Management University, workplace violence from clients or employees feeling angry or hurt is nearly impossible to predict, and having a safety plan in place is in everyone's best interest. She mentions that we owe it to everybody on the veterinary team to take all reasonable precautions to prevent a violent or dangerous workplace situation, whether the circumstance involves a potentially volatile client or an upset employee. You may not think an upset client can turn violent? But all you have to do is look no farther than the internet to read some frightening news headlines.

- *Man Gets 3 Years for Stabbing Vet Workers After Cat Dies*

- *Calgary Vet Physically Assaulted Over Sick Guinea Pig*

- *Man Armed With a Cane Accused of Assaulting Staff, Threatening to Kill Veterinarian*

- *Gunman Threatens Veterinary Staff in Connecticut*

- *Man Beats Up Veterinarian After Dog Dies in Surgery*

- *Dog Owner Arrested After Confrontation With Vet*

- *Florida DVM Assaulted by Distraught Pet Owner*

- *Man Threatens to Bring AK-47 to Veterinarian Office After Cat Dies*

-   *Veterinarian Office Receives Death Threats After Viral Facebook Post*

We recognize that emotions run high because of the human-animal bond and the connection that clients have with their pets, especially during COVID-19 stay-at home orders and with the shift to curbside service and social distancing. We don't interact or connect with clients like we used to. Scenarios we see every day in our practices involve clients being separated from the pets, pets with serious medical conditions, pets who die, and financial concerns. All are potential triggers. Upset clients sometimes blame us when a pet is sick, especially if we cannot see the patient right away, which happens more and more during the pandemic. Add the financial obligation and the situation gets only worse."

Sandy Walsh, The Getting Technical columnist consultant, March 2021, Veterinary Practice Management . . .

Elder Thomas S. Monson said ". . . we are all susceptible to those feelings which, if left unchecked, can lead to anger. We experience displeasure or irritation or antagonism, and if we so choose, we lose our temper and become angry with others. Ironically, those others are often members of our own families—the people we really love the most.

A thoughtful poet gave us this:

A human face I love to view

And trace the passions of the soul;
On it, the spirit writes anew
Each thought and feeling on a scroll.
There the mind its evil doings tells,
And there its noblest deeds do speak;
Just as the ringing of the bells
Proclaims a knell or wedding feast.

Author unknown

Sunflowers And Life

Although we can do it anytime, the beginning of a new year feels like a natural time to reflect upon the past, even as we look forward to the future. It's a chance to leave behind yesterday's regrets, build on yesterday's successes, and look forward to a tomorrow full of potential. There's no reason to doubt that this year can be the best ever. Indeed, when a positive spirit ignites realistic goals, the resulting flame can fuel our efforts to accomplish great things. That doesn't mean we expect the next year to be perfect, of course. None of us knows exactly what is coming, but it's safe to assume that this year, like other years, will have its ups and downs. There will be moments of happiness and joy, along with moments of heartache and worry. Where can we find the courage and perspective to carry on throughout it all? *D. Newel Lloyd, Sunday, January 1, 2017, Music & the Spoken Word.*

Oliver Wendell Holmes stated, "Fame is the scentless sunflower, with gaudy crown of gold; But friendship is the breathing rose, with sweets in every fold." What causes so many to have such a fascination with the sunflower (I'm even allergic to its seeds)? Spending some time looking into this subject I have decided to use some of the sunflower's qualities for my New Year's Resolutions. Below are some of these qualities of the "gaudy sunflower" that I relate to "friendship" and some of the "sweets" I would like to have come my way during 2018:

* Sunflowers are able to grow in the less-than-ideal soil (It's not where you are—it's who you are):—As a child, Marie Curie's family lost their property and fortunes, leaving her and her siblings struggling to get ahead in life. Marie went on to conduct pioneering research on radioactivity. She was the first woman to win a Nobel Prize, the first person (and the only woman) to win twice, and the only person to win twice in multiple sciences.

* Adverse conditions are not able to stop the sunflower (Life's not fair—do your best):—We don't develop courage by being happy every day. We develop it by surviving difficult times and challenging adversity. *Barbara De Angelis.* *Sunflowers not only look at the sun, but they also need a lot of it. They grow best with about 6 to 8 hours a day but more is even better (Look for the light in all you do):—When the sun is shining I can do anything; no mountain is too high, no trouble too difficult to overcome. *Wilma Rudolph.*

* They grow as tall as 16 feet (Stand up and withstand the pricks):—Stand up to your obstacles and do something about them. You will find that they

haven't half the strength you think they have.
Norman Vincent Peale

* Flowers planted too close together will compete and not blossom to their full potential (Give everyone their space and don't suffocate them):—I would rather sit on a pumpkin and have it all to myself than be crowded on a velvet cushion. *Henry David Thoreau.*

* Sunflowers track the sun—the flowers display a behavior called heliotropism. The flower buds and young blossoms will face east in the morning and follow the sun as the earth moves during the day. Then, overnight, they turn east again, ready to greet the next day's light and repeat the cycle (Prepare for tomorrow—it will soon be the present, which is a gift):—Keep your face to the sunshine and you cannot see a shadow. *Helen Keller.*

* There are thousands of tiny flowers in the sunflower's head. Each one of them can produce a seed (There are billions of us and we are all different and special): -Everybody needs beauty as well as bread, places to play in and to pray in, where nature may heal and give strength to the body and soul. *John Muir.*

* As flowers get heavier during seed production, the stems will stiffen and the mature flower heads will generally remain facing east (Getting old is part of nature—be thankful and look to the light):—"Grow old along with me! The best is yet to be, the last of life, for which the first was made. Our times are in his hand who saith, A whole I planned, youth shows but half; Trust God: See all, nor be afraid!" *Robert Browning*.

* They have a history of healing powers (Eternal healing comes through the family):—There was an ingredient used in perfumes and remedies in the Middle Ages called 'momie' that is certainly one of the most fascinating I've come across. *M. J. Rose*.

* They're native to the Americas (We are all native—we are all God's progeny):—The greatest legacy one can pass on to one's children and grandchildren is not money or other material things accumulated in one's life, but rather a legacy of character and faith. *Billy Graham*.

* They were brought to Russia by royalty to be used to produce oil legal to use for lent ("God is no respecter of men" Acts 10:34):—Humility is royalty without a crown. *Spencer W. Kimball*.

* Their popularity stands the test of time (truth is eternal—the right will prevail):—There is only one happiness in this life, to love and be loved. *George Sand*.

* They can be used as scrubbing pads (our bodies are made to use and abuse—and it still is our temple):—You're going to go through tough

times—that's life. But I say, 'Nothing happens to you, it happens for you.' See the positive in negative events. *Joel Osteen.*

Like the young sunflower follows the sun, when we follow the Savior of the world, the Son of God, we flourish and become glorious despite the many terrible circumstances that surround us. He truly is our light and life. *The Lord Is My Light, Elder Quentin L. Cook, April 2015, Ensign.*

Today, while the sun shines, work with a will—

Today all your duties with patience fulfill. Today, while the birds sing, harbor no care—

Call life a good gift, call the world fair. Today, seek the treasure better than gold—

The peace and the joy that are found in the fold. Today, seek the gems that shine in the heart—

While here we labor, choose the better part. Today, seek for goodness, virtue, and truth—

As crown of your life and the grace of your youth. Today, while the heartbeats, live to be true—

Constant and faithful all the way through. Today, today, work with a will—

Today, today, your duties fulfill. Today,
today, work while you may—

Prepare for tomorrow by working today.

"Today while the sun shines", Text: L. Clark, ca.1880,
alt. Music: Evan Stephens, 1854, page 193

We need to give Christ a chance
to make use of us, to be

His word and His work, to share His food and His

clothing in the world today.

If we do not radiate the

light of Christ around us, the sense of the darkness that

prevails in the world will increase.

Mother Teresa

Divine Intervention

An event can be considered as Divine Intervention when the Lord chooses to influence events and circumstances in an unusual or unexpected way. Things fall into place or unrelated things come together or circumstances change sufficiently that the outcome is changed. Things turn out differently than we would have otherwise expected. Some of the examples of when the Lord intervened are:

- Joseph was sold into Egypt by his brothers, but the Lord, through a series of events, eventually brought him to a position where he could save his family from famine. (Genesis 37:39-46)

- Moses perform 10 plagues against the Pharaoh. (Ex 7:19-11:10; 12:29-30)

- The Lord gave Joshua direction on how to bring down the walls of Jericho and begin the conquest of the promised land. (Joshua 6)

We must be cautious and keep in mind that just because there are simultaneous occurrences of two events does not prove that they are related or that one caused the other or are of Divine Intervention. Gerald N. Lund stated, "I remember many years ago reading in the newspaper of a major power outage in New York City. Huge areas of the city were blacked out for long hours. A few days later I learned about a young boy who had been walking home at that very time. He had a stick and as he passed a line of telephone poles, he took a good solid whack at each one. At the very moment he struck one of the poles, the power went out. Frightened at what he had 'done,' he ran home and hid in his room. He was certain that when the police discovered his part in all this, he would end up in jail. Only later, when the power came back on, did his parents learn why he was so afraid to go out again." Gerald N. Lund, Hearing the Voice of the Lord, 2007 pg 113.

In 1969 I was attending Purdue University and it was embroiled in a debate over who would win the college football 1970 Heisman Trophy:

- There was one Joe Theismann playing football for Notre Dame from South River, New Jersey who pronounced his last name Thees-man. At the beginning of the 1970 football season Roger Valdiserri, Notre Dame's sports information director, asked Joe if his last name should be pronounced Theismann in a way that rhymed with Heisman. Mr. Theismann said no but why would you ask? He said, "I want to tell you something.

There's a trophy out there called the Heisman Trophy. It goes to the best college player in the country. We think you have a chance to win that trophy. But we're not just going to count on your athletic ability, nor the reputation of the University of Notre Dame. But we think by just simply changing the pronunciation of your last name from THEES-mann to THIGHS-mann to rhyme with Heisman, we can get you that trophy."

- There was another college football player by the name of Jim Plunkett. He was born in San Jose, California, and played for Stanford University. He grew up in a poor household and his parent's financial condition was extremely weak, they received state financial aid, and his father was a news vendor who had to support his blind wife along with his three children. His father died of a heart attack in 1969.

I know at Purdue University, and I had the impression all around the country, the campaigning of the slogan "Theismann for Heisman" didn't sit well. Anyway, Jim Plunkett won the Heisman Trophy and Joe Theismann was second in the balloting and they both went on to have great quarterback careers.

I had my False Devine Intervention experience on Monday, Nov. 18, 1985, during a Monday Night Football game between the New York Giants and Joe Theismann's Washington Red Skins. I was driving home from work, listening to the football game, and Joe was moving the ball down the field. Somewhere in the back of my mind, the memory of "Theismann for Heisman" chants made me blurt out, "Can't anyone stop him? Why doesn't someone break his leg." And, on the next play, his leg was broken with a career-ending injury. That moment has carried with me to this day. I know that God would not have granted little old me such a wish and I know that it was a coincidental event. But, I have since that night been moved to be more thoughtful in my wishes.

Joseph B. Wirthlin said, "Kindness is the essence of celestial life, kindness is how a Christlike person treats others. Kindness should permeate all of our words and actions at work, at school, at church, and especially in our homes."

*"Be careful for what you wish for,
you may receive it."*

W. W. Jacobs

Sheep vs Goats

The consensus of man states that goats are more intelligent, independent, curious, mischievous, and smarter than sheep. Compared to sheep they will escape from their enclosure, can be trouble makers, and aggressive towards their family as well as man. They can adapt themselves with the environment easier than sheep. Goats tend to scatter when alarmed where sheep tend to run if spooked or approached and they are most comfortable with their flock. Sheep like to graze on grass. On the other hand, goats like to graze on almost everything they can reach and find edible (leaves, plants, twigs, etc.).

Matthew 25: 31-33 mentions that in the final days of judgment Christ will place the sheep on His right side and the goats on the left. And in John 1:9, 3:20 He discusses that every man is born with the light of Christ and they that do evil hate the light. There isn't much more written in the Bible indicating why Christ will place the sheep on his right side and the goats on His left. I guess that those on His left will use as one of their reasons that "the devil made them do it." I'm not very familiar with sheep or goats but I did raise a bum lamb.

Many, many, many years ago, my mother got me
a bum lamb, she may have felt sorry for the orphan,
or was concerned that I needed more responsibility
or would turn out to not be worth a damn.
Along with the lamb, there was a bottle and nipple,
and to me, at that age, it all seemed quite simple.
I think her name was Agatha but my sister thinks
it was Daisy Mae, either way,
she and I loved to romp and play.
She would push the nursing bottle against my
stomach hard, and the way she ate reminded me of
Miss Royal Charm IV my pet New Hampshire hog.
And as she suckled the bottle, her long limp tail wagged
rapidly hanging down between her rear legs. Like my dog
Judy's happy tail, only Judy held her tail up like a dog.
She didn't seem stupid as they say about sheep,
I kind of fell in love with her and to me, she was unique.
And I became very depressed when I realized we got her at
least partly to have lamb meat to consume.
And for the long term, to keep her at
home there was just not enough room.
To make a long story short my mom heard my pleas,
and she found a sheepherder who would take her
after I think she got onto both of her knees.
Several years later the sheepherder got a hold of my mom
and said my lamb's life had been productive and long.
In fact she had become a leader sheep for his flock,
and in a Snake River flood, a little like in 1976 when the

Idaho Snake River Teton Dam broke,
with a rope around her
neck followed the herder as they led his sheep off an island.
And he noticed that no sheep were lost
as he secured the gate with a lock.
WOW—a famous sheep was raised by me that
saved scores of sheep in a flood,
a sheep that allowed itself to be led by
its owner and was not a dud.
Now I wonder what would happen if the
leader of the sheep was a GOAT?
Knowing what I know about SHEEP and GOATS,
I suspect the curious old GOAT would hang himself
with the lead rope.

Walter R. Hoge, written for Shauna
on our tenth wedding anniversary
called Sheep vs Goats in recognition
that 2015 the Chinese New Year was
celebrated as the YEAR OF THE GOAT

Christ did say, ". . . them on the left hand, Depart
from me ye cursed"—Best not to be a Goat?

Recently a runaway sheep who spent many years in the Australian bush was found with so much wool that he struggled to remain upright and could barely see. The rescued sheep was shorn of 78 pounds of wool. The shelter commented, "We truly believe that he understands . . . we have eased his life and turned it for the better." Bet a goat can't top that either. *The Week, 03/19/2021.*

Honey Bees Attraction To Sugar

Elder M. Russell Ballard wrote, "Father loved his gentle honeybees and marveled at the way thousands of them working together transformed the nectar gathered from his peach blossoms into sweet, golden honey—one of nature's most beneficial foods. In fact, nutritionists tell us it is one of the foods that includes all the substances—enzymes, vitamins, minerals, and water—necessary to sustain life. My father always tried to involve me in his work with his hives, but I was very happy to let him tend to his bees. However, since those days, I have learned more about the highly organized beehive—a colony of about 60,000 bees. Honeybees are driven to pollinate, gather nectar, and condense the nectar into honey. It is their magnificent obsession imprinted into their genetic makeup by our Creator. It is estimated that to produce just one pound (0.45 kg) of honey, the average hive of 20,000 to 60,000 bees must collectively visit millions of flowers and travel the equivalent of two times around the world. Over its short lifetime of just a few weeks to four months, a single honeybee's contribution of honey to its hive is a mere one-twelfth of one teaspoon. Though seemingly insignificant when compared to the total, each bee's one-twelfth of a teaspoon of honey is vital to the life of the hive. The bees depend on each other. Work that would be overwhelming for a few bees to do becomes lighter because all of the bees faithfully do their part. *November 2012, Ensign, Be Anxiously Engaged, Elder M. Russell Ballard of the Quorum of the Twelve Apostles.*

Honey bees are known to communicate through many different chemicals and odors, as is common in insects, but also using specific behaviors such as dances that convey information about the quality and type of resources in the environment, and where these resources are located. The details of the signaling being used vary from species to species; for example, the two smallest species, Apis andreniformis and A. florea, dance on the upper surface of the comb, which is horizontal (not vertical, as in other species), and worker bees orient the dance in the actual compass direction of the resource to which they are recruiting. *Wikipedia.*

In the *October 29, 2016, Science News on page 12 Clint Perry (neurologist at Queen Mary University of London)* states, "Scientists can't ask animals how they feel. Instead, researchers must look for signs of positive or negative emotions in an animal's behavior. In one such study, for example, scientists shook bees vigorously in a machine for 60 seconds—hard enough to annoy but not to injure . . . and found that stressed bees made more pessimistic decisions while foraging . . . But when the scientists gave half the bees a treat—sugar water . . . the results suggested that the bees had not only experienced an energy boost from the sugar but were in a more positive, optimistic state."

A writer in the Huffington Post mentioned, "Many of you have probably heard of the old adage, 'You can catch more flies with honey than vinegar.' This was one of the first rules of life that my mother taught me, and you'd better believe I have perfected it. I learned at a very young age that life was just easier if you put a smile on your face instead of a scowl when approaching the world. Along with this lesson I learned to let the little things go. If someone did something that could be perceived as rude, I would just flash them a smile and carry on. Someone emailed me recently with the same sentiment, saying, "Being nice to nice people is great, but being nice to those who are not nice to you is how the world becomes better. We should not want to defeat or humiliate those we don't agree with but to win their friendship and understanding." *You Can Catch More Flies With Honey Than Vinegar, The Huffington Post, Feb 2002.*

At bedtime when my five children were very young they would all lay on a bed with me and ask me to tell them a story. They would often ask me to tell them about a fantasy land (McEaster Valley) where Mr. and Mrs. McEaster lived. As stated by them, "Our mission is to try to help those on planet earth direct their attention, at least one day a year, toward their creator and what He has done for us. We accomplish this task by doing caring and fun things in such a way that everyone can participate. Their attention may be toward nature and its gift of life, or towards the Savior and his giving of his life for us so that we may have the gift of life. Or their attention may just be placed towards the family having a fun-filled day with hidden gifts, candy, and toys." I always included myself in these stories and there I was able to find a special place that I wanted my life to be like. As I look back at sharing these adventures with my children this was my "spoon full of sugar". At the end of the book, I later wrote, Mr. McEaster tells me, ". . . that I had not stumbled into their valley. The residents had spent a long time choosing me. They wanted me to stay and dedicate my talents to their cause, and the reward I could expect was the feeling one has when he gives service without recognition. If I came, it would be permanent; I would not taste death. I would look aged on the outside but eternally young in mind, body, and soul. I was educated in a profession that they needed, and I seemed to love my work and had been consistent in my ethics. I had not shown any signs of growing up. I seemed to sing and dance and play my days away on a regular basis, and my downs didn't seem to last long. I seemed to be tolerant of others and usually didn't get in the way of the creativity or contributions they made." *Easter: McEaster Valley, W.R. Hoge, 2010.*

"In every job that must be done there is an element of fun you find the fun, and snap! The job's a game and every task you undertake becomes a piece of cake. A lark, a spree! . . . The honeybees that fetch the nectar from the flowers to the comb never tire of ever buzzing to and fro. Because they take a little nip from every flower that they sip and hence they find their task is not a grind . . . It's very clear to see: That a spoonful of sugar helps the medicine

go down . . . in a most delightful way." *Marry Poppins.*
May we f ind our "spoon full of sugar" that not only helps us
experience an energy boost from the sugar but also "a more
positive, optimistic state."

.

My Prostate Cancer Therapy

The radioisotope Radium was first discovered in 1898 by Marie and Pierre Curie, after they extracted a single milligram from ten tons of a uranium ore called pitchblende. And it was pretty darn cool. It glowed, and seriously, how exciting is that? It didn't take long for entrepreneurs to see the potential value in the luminescent properties of radium. Just a few years after its discovery zinc sulfide was mixed with it to create paint. The people who worked with it would glow as they walked through the streets at night. It wasn't until 1914 that radium-based luminescent paint started to be produced in the US. By 1921, they weren't just making paints, they were doing the painting, too. Scores of young women, as young as 11-years-old, were hired to paint watch dials with the glow-in-the-dark, radium-based paint. They were also encouraged to put the brush between their lips and twirl it into a point. It was the best way to get truly precise numbers and brush strokes. It was thought to be super healthy: it was often marketed as a cure-all, and there was a shocking number of products that hit the market just full of radium. People drank radium water and brushed their teeth with radium toothpaste, and radium cosmetics were all the rage. Children played with toys painted with radium, and performers on the New York stage danced and twirled in costumes that glowed. Early experiments using radium to kill cancer cells had been a success. Doctors started experimenting with it as a cure for things like tuberculosis, lupus, and everything from acne and baldness to impotence and insanity.

During veterinary school in 1972, I took a class and was certified to work with radioisotopes, like Radium. I used this knowledge as part of my research with thyroid functions tests. The results of these experiments standardized lab tests using thyroid-stimulating hormone (TSH). In 2014 I developed prostate cancer and guess what? Treatments for this cancer include x-ray and radioisotope radiation as well as the sex hormones that I worked with during graduate school. Discussing the progression of my disease we decided to go "all out" for a cure. I was given a sex hormone injection, pills, had radioactive (radioisotopes) pellets placed in my prostate gland, and a series of treatments of concentrated x-ray beams directed at my prostate. It was like graduate and veterinary school all over again. The only difference was that I was the research animal. I monitored the effects the hormones had on my body (mostly weakness from loss of muscle mass, fatigue, and hot flashes), monitored the radioisotope pellets with a Geiger counter (caused frequent urination), and concentrated external beams x-ray radiation directed at the prostate and as little exposure to other tissues in the surrounding areas (needed to be held still in a mold made of my body—treatments lasted about

7 weeks). The treatments appear to have been successful but the consequences of treatment aren't much appreciated. According to statistics with no treatment, I would be in a lot of pain or have left this planet by now. Life vs pain or death—life is a good choice. To celebrate my planned treatment, I sent all my family a letter explaining what I would probably be going through along with a beautiful piece of antique uranium table serving glass that was produced from adding the fluorescent uranium to melted glass. Production of glass was stopped sharply because of shortages of uranium during the Cold War in the 1940s to 1990s. It glows green with a black light like Halloween decorations.

Perhaps unsurprisingly, there were no safety precautions put in place for working with this Radium discovered by Marie Curie that we now know is deadly. The military was even signing contracts to paint watches and instrument panels, which meant more work for the girls. Radium gets absorbed into the bones and when that happens, the rot starts. They started to find a whole host of symptoms. Some started suffering from chronic exhaustion. For many, it started with their teeth—one by one, those teeth would start to decay and rot. When they were removed, their gums wouldn't heal. In some cases, the jaw would just simply disintegrate at the dentist's touch. Bad breath was common. Skin became so delicate that the slightest touch would tear open wounds. Ulcers formed for some, and those that were pregnant bore stillborn babies. Unfortunately, unless radiation is concentrated it usually goes undetected. We get radiation exposure from the cosmic planetary bodies, from soil water, and vegetation, elements such as potassium-40, carbon-14 and lead- 210, and manmade materials such as tobacco, televisions, medical x-rays, smoke detectors, lantern mantles, nuclear medicine, building materials, the list goes on.

Richard G. Scott wrote, "Years ago I participated in the measurement of the nuclear characteristics of different materials. The process used an experimental nuclear reactor designed so that high-energy particles streamed from a hole in the center of the reactor. These particles were directed into an experimental chamber where measurements were made. The high-energy particles could not be seen, but they had to be carefully controlled to avoid harm to others. One day a janitor entered while we were experimenting. In a spirit of disgust, he said, "You are all liars, pretending that you are doing something important but you can't fool me. I know that if you can't see, hear, taste, smell, or touch it, it doesn't exist." That attitude ruled out the possibility of his learning that there is much of worth that can't be identified by the five senses. Had that man been willing to open his mind to understand how the presence of nuclear particles is detected, he would have confirmed their existence. In like manner, never doubt the reality of faith. The axiom "You get what you pay for" is true for spiritual rewards as well as temporal concerns. You get what you pay for in obedience, in faith in Jesus Christ, in the diligent application of the truths that you learn. What you get is the molding of your character, with growth in capacity, and the successful completion of your purpose here on earth, which is to grow through being proven." *Richard G. Scott, 21 Principles, Divine Truths To Help You Live By The Spirit, page 97.*

The girls who have become known as the "society of the living dead" weren't aided by their community—they were shunned. In spite of the fact that these were young mothers, wives, and girls who were dying, the communities they lived in just didn't want to acknowledge what was happening to them. Ottawa, Illinois was known as Death City throughout the 1930s and in 1987, a documentary tried to show just how long-lasting the effects were, in a very graphic way: when one man headed into the Catholic cemetery that is the final resting place of many of the Radium Girls, the Geiger counter he carried goes nuts—their remains, six feet down, are still radioactive. The half-life of Radium is 1600 years. With some of the girls, precautions were taken over concerns of radiation admissions and they were buried in lead-lined coffins. Industrialist and golfer Eben Byers was the poster child for a drink called RadiThor, and drank several bottles of it a day. Holes formed in his skull, his jaw fell off, and his bones began to crumble. He died in 1932 and was so radioactive that he too was buried in a lead-lined coffin. *The Radium Girls, Shutterstock, Debra Kelly, 07/14/2020.*

I grew up within 60 miles of the Atomic Energy Commission near Arco Idaho where nuclear reactor power was first used in 1951 to produce electricity and lived in a home where my parents built a bomb shelter. I was frightened in my youth by movies (as an eight-year-old "Creature from the Black Lagoon" gave me nightmares for months. For some reason I thought the creature was a result of radiation mutations—maybe the 3D viewing had the most effect.). My fear of nuclear bombs was raised during the Cuban Missile Crisis of 1962, living near Arco Idaho, and the stories I was told, true or fiction, about the potential death and destruction from radiation. In 1969 as a new graduate student at Purdue University walking downstairs into underground offices, I noticed a civil defense-looking sign on the stairs that stated what should be done in case of a nuclear attack. Flashes of the fears and anxieties I grew up with as a child over the development of a nuclear bomb made me stop and read the sign. A smile came to my face as I read on the last line the only entirely true statement: "Then kiss your ass goodbye!"

Realities in the Life
of a Veterinarian

I n 1972 the United States Department of Agriculture (USDA) established the Animal and Plant Health Inspection Service. In the spring of 1973, my veterinary graduating class was one of the first to receive the new training and examination qualifying us to examine and sign health certificates allowing healthy animals to legally travel between states and countries. During that time a classmate and I had arranged job hunting visits in California. We found opportunities in the San Francisco Bay Area and upon returning to Indiana were informed that we had missed training and needed to take the exam. We found ourselves doing self-study and the anxiety of taking the test of the new regulations without any guidance from the USDA. Also, before graduation ceremonies, we filled out an application to hold a Controlled Substance Registration Certificate issued by the United States Department of Justice, Drug Enforcement Administration (DEA). They describe their mission as ". . . whether compounds are illicit drugs such as cocaine, heroin, methamphetamine, or legitimately produced pharmaceuticals, they must all be manufactured.

Many problems associated with drug abuse are the result of legitimately made controlled substances being diverted from their lawful purpose into illicit drug traffic. The mission of DEA's Diversion Control Division is to prevent, detect, and investigate the diversion of controlled pharmaceuticals and listed chemicals from legitimate sources while ensuring an adequate and uninterrupted supply for legitimate medical, commercial, and scientific needs." During my career as a veterinary practice owner, the DEA has been a hammer over my head. Records of the quantity of drugs purchased, dispensed to pet owners, or used in the hospital needed to match. Also, only qualified staff members were allowed to access guarded secure drug storage areas and special request forms were needed to purchase these drugs. With all this effort to be sure medications are used properly a study in 2019 by Auburn University found "Veterinarians and veterinary technicians or technologists had significantly higher rates of death by suicide, compared with findings for the general population, whereas veterinary assistants or laboratory animal caretakers did not." The study also noted that this might be attributable to pentobarbital access, a drug used for the humane euthanasia of animals.

In December 1957, Frankie Lymon appeared on "The Ed Sullivan Show" to sing "Goody Goody," nearly two years after "Why Do Fools Fall in Love?" was a hit debut single. That voice! Those apple cheeks! Arms wide, head back, he radiates joy. That beautiful soprano flying high, talent and presence, and just enough ham to sell it all. And it was a great story, too: Up from nothing! A shooting star! So, when they found Frankie Lymon dead at the age of

25 one February morning in 1968, in the same apartment building where he'd grown up, it was the end of something and the beginning of something, but no one was quite sure what. Frankie Lymon and the Teenagers were five kids from Washington Heights, just north of Harlem. They sang doo-wop under the streetlight on the corner of 165th and Amsterdam. They were discovered by Valentines' lead singer Richie Barrett while the kids were rehearsing in an apartment house. A few months later their first record, "Why Do Fools Fall in Love?" made it to the top of the national charts. It was 1956. Overnight, Frankie Lymon was the hottest singer in America, off on a world tour. He was 13 years old.

That made him the first black teenage pop star, a gaptoothed, baby-faced, angel-voiced paragon of show business ambition, and a camera-ready avatar of America's new postwar youth movement. He was a founding father of rock 'n' roll even before his voice had changed. That voice and that style influenced two generations of rock, soul, and R&B giants. You heard his echoes everywhere. The high, clear countertenor, like something out of Renaissance church music, found its way from the Temptations to the Beach Boys to Earth, Wind & Fire. Even Diana Ross charted a cover of "Why Do Fools Fall in Love?" Unfortunately, Frankie Lymon grew up too fast in every way imaginable. "I never was a child, although I was billed in every theater and auditorium where I appeared as a child star," Lymon told Art Peters, a reporter for Ebony magazine, in 1967. "I was a man when I was 11 years old, doing everything that most men do. In the neighborhood where I lived, there was no time to be a child. There were five children in my family and my folks had to scuffle to make ends meet. My father was a truck driver and my mother worked as a domestic in white folks' homes. While kids my age were playing stickball and marbles, I was working in the corner grocery store carrying orders to help pay the rent."

Nobody makes it through life without making mistakes. Some are harmless, but others can be dangerous. Most often, safety lies in being cautious and wise. We don't usually get into trouble without disregarding a rule of safety or some code of behavior. Danger lurks on the other side of a warning. Maybe it's a No Trespassing or Use Caution sign; it could be the small print on a bottle or perhaps a trail marker or even an unsettled feeling. Whatever form the warning takes, it can save us from a lot of trouble.

Kenny, a fictional fourth-grader in Christopher Paul Curtis's book The Watsons Go to Birmingham, learned this lesson well. On a hot summer day in Alabama, Kenny could not resist the temptation to go swimming, despite the No Swimming sign and warnings about a whirlpool. But Kenny could see no danger, so he decided to swim anyway. At first, he was only going to step in the water, but when he caught sight of a turtle, he decided to swim toward it. Before he knew it, he was caught in the vicious whirlpool. Reflecting on his near-death experience, the boy said: "There's one good thing about getting in trouble: It seems like you do it in steps . . . It also seems like the worse the trouble is that you get into, the more steps it takes to get there. Sort of like you're getting a bunch of little warnings on the way; sort of like if you really wanted to you could turn around." Whether the danger is a whirlpool (a place from where you may never return) or something less tangible, we can choose to avoid precarious situations by being wise enough to heed warnings. Seek out and listen to the counsel of those who have gone before. Find safety in prudent laws, rules, commandments, and guideposts. See them not as restrictions but as welcome warnings that keep us out of harm's way. Even if we think we know better, as Kenny did, chances are we'll be glad we paid attention to the "little warnings on the way." *The Watsons Go to Birmingham—1963 (1995), 173. Music & the Spoken Word #4213.*

Not feeling that you need to follow laws, rules, or guideposts and that it's okay to sin a little is like a journey that begins with the first step. "It also seems like the worse the trouble is that you get into, the more steps it takes to get there." And we soon learn from wisdom and experience that it is easier to resist the first temptation than later ones when a pattern of transgression has begun to develop.

Unfortunately, at the age of eleven Frankie Lyman had ignored many warning steps if he was "a man . . . doing everything that most men do." At the age of fifteen, he had been sucked into the whirlpool and Frankie was a heroin addict. He tried to kick, tried again and again, and got straight for a while. But, ask any junkie and they'll tell what they're chasing is the feeling they got the first time they got high. But that first-time rush can never be recaptured, whether you're talking about heroin or cigarettes or hit records. Then his mother died, and he fell hard. He wasn't alone. Heroin was everywhere in New York by then, and methadone clinics run by the city were springing up in neighborhoods all over town. The failure rate was heartbreaking. "I looked twice my age," Lymon told Ebony. "I was thin as a shadow and I didn't give a damn. My only concern was in getting relief. You know, an addict is the most pathetic creature on earth. He knows that every time he sticks a needle in his arm, he's gambling with death and, yet, he's got to have it. It's like playing Russian Roulette with a spike. There's always the danger that some peddler will sell him a poisoned batch—some garbage." Here young Frankie knocks on wood. "I was lucky. God must have been watching over me."

There has been a tongue-in-cheek statement made over the years among veterinarians, "Every veterinarian should be given a bottle of pentobarbital at his retirement dinner." Thoughts about what may await us as geriatric diseases set in may lead to thoughts of an easy way out. A sad story from such a thought occurred with a veterinarian in our area years ago who had problems that he could not see a solution to. He went home one evening, placed a catheter in his arm, and injected himself with a lethal dose of pentobarbital leaving a wife and young family behind.

"... they found Frankie Lymon dead at the age of 25 one February morning in 1968, in the same apartment building where he'd grown up ..."

The Dromedary Camel

During my studies at the College of Veterinary Medicine at Purdue University, a camel was admitted into the large animal clinics from a circus with a broken neck. I remember the instructor assigned to the animal's care commenting that he was able to take x-rays of the camel's neck, determine that it was broken but had no idea of where to go from there. Many years later one of my clients, Norma Tucker, at Camden Pet Hospital offered me the opportunity to buy 50% of a camel that she would like to care for at her ranch. She felt it would be great for my young children to make the long trip on winding roads off of Hick's Road into the Santa Cruz mountains and ride her horses and the camel. This might have been a great opportunity for me to bond with my children and become a super dad for the moment; however, being very busy trying to manage a hospital and make payments on a clinic, veterinary hospital, and home, I felt this would be another great idea that would not sustain itself for very long. So, by not taking the bait from my client, I lost the chance to gain experiences the Purdue instructor could only dreamed of.

Camels originated in North America and migrated to Asia over the land bridge that once existed. They subsequently died out in North America, though the camel family is still represented in South America, with the alpaca, llama, and vicuna. Early in US history, most expansions occurred from the eastern US to the west. At the time, most of the land west of the Mississippi was wild and lawless. There were also numerous skirmishes between the settlers and various Indian tribes. To help with these issues, the US Army, specifically the cavalry, established several forts throughout the west.

One of the problem areas was the desert southwest. The cavalry used horses, but they could only go to places that had available water for the horses to drink and enough food for them to eat. The desert areas were not good for either food or water, but there was a definite need. In the early 1800s, a proposal was made to purchase and import some camels. It was noted that camels are capable of traveling long distances without food and water and that they could also maintain a steady pace for days, while horses needed rest much more frequently. In 1855, Congress approved the expenditure of $30,000 to acquire some camels and in all, 33 camels were purchased from Egypt, Turkey, and Tunisia. By February 1857, the camel herd had grown to 70 animals and these were stationed at Camp Verde, Texas. The advantages of camels over horses and wagons were quickly seen and many people fully supported the expansion of what had become the Camel Corps. A number of camels were moved to Camp Tejon in California and it is quite possible that the camel corps would have expanded even more, had it not been for the American Civil War. In particular, the Confederate Army captured Camp Verde, though Camp Tejon remained in Union control. None of the camels were used during the war. After the war, the new secretary of war, Edwin Stanton, who was unaware of how useful camels were and could be, ordered the camels to be sold. They were and many of the people who bought them ended up abandoning the animals or purposely turned them loose. The last official sighting of wild camels in the southwest deserts was in the 1940s. *Did You Know That There are Camels in the United States? By Rex Trulove, 2018.*

The dromedary camel has one hump on its back. It is filled with about eighty pounds of fat that can be used for fuel when food is scarce. As the fat is used for energy, the hump gets smaller and begins to tip to one side. The hump quickly builds back to normal when the camel gets proper rest and a good food supply. In a long day, the dromedary camel can carry a four hundred pound load a hundred miles across a hot, dry desert. They have been known to go eight days without drinking water and can become quite dehydrated. They may lose as much as 227 pounds of body weight and the ribs will show through the skin. The camel can drink as much as twenty-seven gallons of water in ten minutes and the stomach will be empty in another ten minutes. The water has been absorbed from the stomach by blood vessels and carried to all parts of the body. Therefore, the camel's body can rehydrate in a very short period of time. The camel can lose 40% of its water and remain healthy. If a man loses 5% (he can't see), 10% (he can't hear and will go insane), and 12% of his body water and his heart will stop. It is believed the camel's elongated red blood cells make it possible for them to become so dehydrated. The camel conserves water by having a nose that when breathing traps warm, moist air from the lungs and absorbs it into tiny blood vessels in the nasal membranes. This can be accomplished because the nose remains cooler than the warm moist air from the lungs. The nose stays as much as 18 degrees cooler than the rest of the body from breathing in hot desert air through moist nasal passages. Camels have special muscles in their nostrils that can close the openings, keeping sand out of the nose but still allowing them enough air to breathe during dust storms. The dromedary camel's feet consist of two long, bony toes with a tough, leathery skin between. The hooves are wide and get wider with the skin between them when they are stepped on. They form a webbed appearance a little like a duck. The result is that the feet will not sink into the soft, drifting sand allowing them to walk about ten miles an hour. When they are six months of age tough thick knee pads start to grow on the front legs that allow them to lower their 1000 pounds to the ground without getting sores or infected areas on their knees. The eyelashes arch down over the eyes like screens, keeping the sand and the bright sun out but still allowing them to see clearly. If sand gets in the eye, there is an inner eyelid that acts like a windshield wiper that automatically wipes the sand off the eyeball. The camel walks with its head held high and the nose in the air. This is because the eyebrows are so thick and bushy that they need to peek underneath them to see.

Besides the ability a camel has to carry heavy loads for long distances without needing much food or water it provides very rich milk that is used to make into butter and cheese, its thick hair coat is shed once a year and can be woven into cloth and young camel are used to provide meat. And, when the dromedary camel is hungry it places little pressure on its owner for food. It can eat almost anything. Its mouth is so tough that a leather bridle, piece of rope, tent material, or thorny cacti don't bother it. It can survive on grass and other plants found in the Arabian desert. *National Geographic Magazine & others.*

In the Bible it talks about a multitude of camels (from the eastern trading tribes) that will cover you (Jerusalem), The young camels of Midian and Ephah; All those from Sheba (who once came to trade) will come Bringing gold and frankincense. And proclaiming the praises of the Lord (Jesus Christ)—Isaiah 60:6. This refers to the long journey the Magi (wise men) would make following the star to worship and give gifts of great worth to the newborn king. The gifts given were:

-   Gold- This precious metal has been a sign of royalty, wealth, and power since mankind began. It's been used as a form of currency for centuries. It represents Jesus as King of Kings (Kingship).

-   Frankincense- was used in the temple for incense, anointing oil, and perfumes. It is a type of resin from tree sap that creates a white smoke when burned. It represents Jesus as God and a High Priest (Diety).

- Myrrh- Myrrh like Frankincense is also a gum risen from the Myrrh tree. It starts coming out of the tree as oil but starts to harden when exposed to air. It gets its name from Marar which means bitterness. Most Bible teachers and preachers share how myrrh symbolizes the death and burial that Jesus would have to face on the cross and many believe that it goes deeper! For myrrh to be cultivated it must be extracted by piercing the tree's heartwood and allowing the gum to trickle out into bitter red droplets called tears. It represents the sacrifice Jesus would face to the point of dying on the cross. (Suffering).

A camel is not a pretty animal, nor is it known for its good behavior. It is one of the most awkward of all domestic animals and among the most difficult to manage. It has several bad habits, such as biting people or animals and spitting on strangers. Still, this animal is very useful to desert dwellers where it is known as "the ship of the desert." I'm sure the camel over the centuries has carried more valuable merchandise on their back than any other animal on the planet.

Since I spent a good share of my life trying to encourage my children to show good behavior, learn some grace, be cooperative when working with others, not acquiring bad habits, and not bite or spit on anyone—it was probably a good choice not to invest in a camel with my client living in the Santa Cruz Mountains . . .

My Personal Miracle

E lder Dallin H. Oaks stated, "A miracle has been defined as 'a beneficial event brought about through divine power that mortals do not understand and of themselves cannot duplicate.' The idea that events are brought about through divine power is rejected by most irreligious people and even by some who are religious. All of us have known people who have what Elder Neal A. Maxwell of the Quorum of the Twelve Apostles once called 'the anti-miracle mindset.' This rejection of miracles in the last days was prophesied. The prophet Nephi foretold that the Gentiles would 'put down the power and miracles of God, and preach up unto themselves their own wisdom and their own learning, that they may get gain' (2 Ne. 26:20). He also prophesied that churches would be built up in which persons would teach with their learning, deny the power of God, and tell the people that if someone should 'say there is a miracle wrought by the hand of the Lord, believe it not; for this day he is not a God of miracles' (2 Ne. 28:6)." Some people reject the possibility of miracles because they have not experienced them or cannot understand them. In contrast, President Howard

W. Hunter declared, 'To deny the reality of miracles on the ground that the results and manifestations must be fictitious simply because we cannot comprehend the means by which they have happened is arrogant on the face of it'."
Miracles, Dallin Oaks Elder Dallin H. Oaks, Of the Quorum of the Twelve Apostles, Ensign, June 2001, p 6.

I would like to share with you an experience I have had that confirmed to me that miracles do happen. In 1995 my father, an MD- general practitioner & Surgeon, sent me a copy of a letter he had written to Dr. Petersen, a urologist specialist, in Salt Lake City about his prostate cancer. Dad's letter, being a medical doctor himself, caught my attention. One would not expect a doctor to write a letter to another doctor about himself. I also would not expect words such as "my thoughts, fears, present situation, scared me etcetera." I read the letter and looked at my father's PSA (an indicator for prostate cancer). The numbers alarmed me, I called dad and we discussed a few things about how he was doing and I relayed that he was in our thoughts and prayers. Dad's prostate cancer was brought under control by using hormone therapy and the letter was forgotten after dad passed—not from prostate cancer.

When it comes to taking care of my own health I used to do a lot of self-care—monitor my blood pressure, blood glucose, PSA, and exercise programs. I began to notice increased elevations in my PSA test results that I would send to mail-in laboratories. I was sure that I hadn't taken the tests correctly or that they weren't handled properly through the mail. I was committing a sin of omission by putting it off, self-denial. In 2013 (eighteen years after my dad had sent me a copy of his letter) I was in my messy garage and for some reason pulled open an old file cabinet drawer that I had not touched for years. The drawer was stuffed with things I had saved from my dad's personal affects that had interested me. As I pulled hard on the drawer, the letter I've referred to above, came out of the drawer and fell at my feet. Nothing else came out of the drawer.

Because of that letter, I was stimulated to have my prostate checked. I had an elevated PSA, biopsies tested positive for cancer, and cell types indicated that some were likely to become metastatic (if they hadn't already) and that I needed to make some decisions about my health and soon. Because of that letter and the "miracle" hint given to me, I'm sure from my Father in Heaven, I have not shown any cancer signs since my treatment. I haven't been fully aware of how lucky I was until recently I have been watching a friend dying of the disease.

God lives and He watches over us and will guide and direct us into happiness and joy if we live in such a way to receive, recognize and heed his promptings. "Consider the song God moves in a mysterious way." We won't understand everything that happens in our life, but we can be sure God will take care of us. *Hymn "God Moves in a Mysterious Way", William Cowper (1731-1800). "God moves in a mysterious way, yes His wonders to perform"*

Dr. Florence Chambers & Letter to My Neurologist
Dr. . . .
Director Stroke Center
2577 Samaritan Drive, #840
San Jose, CA 95124

Dr. . . . , Approximately eight years ago I began writing monthly letters to my special need's clients (loss of a family member or one with dementia, cancer, alone, loss of a special pet, etc.) and my children. The main reason for writing was for my clients that I have known for many years—but I also wanted to somehow help my posterity know something about my life when I'm gone and they start wondering more about who they are, where they came from, and where they are headed. I know that writing a journal would more than likely have little impact on their interest so I write these letters in hopes that someday these stories will catch their interest and they will learn more about my thoughts and feelings. This activity also keeps me always looking for something of interest to share and hopefully will keep the plasticity of my brain alert and active.

Enclosed is a letter I recently sent out to my family and friends about my mom's smiley face drawing and the song she taught me that has helped me over the years. I currently give this picture to my clients that are down, have kids at home, or other needs. Last week a seventy-seven-year-old client grabbed it from my hand when I asked her if she really wanted to see what my mother had drawn in the '50s.

I have thought of the care you give patients that are often in much more need of a lift than the clients I see. So, I decided to give you a copy of the drawing, words to the song and the letter I sent. Nothing is under copy protection—maybe a copy shared might help brighten someone's day.

I also wonder if I would have known that the picture was a smiley/frowny face when I was trying to remember the name clip as you were pointing it out on your pen after I had my stroke (04/23/2019). Also, FYI I have a difficult time remembering the names of people and things. When I was a teenager one day I was sitting in my father's office (who was an MD) and a psychiatrist, Dr. Florence Chambers, working in dad's clinic called me into her office. She said, "Mr. Hoge I understand you have trouble remembering people's names." You can imagine how intimidated I must have felt. After a short visit that seemed forever to me, she said, "Mr. Hoge don't worry about not remembering names. You will remember things that are important in your life and do just fine."

I understand Einstein had such a bad memory that he once lost his ticket on a train and the ticket taker, knowing him, trusting that he had boughten a ticket. He asked him where his stop was and Einstein couldn't even remember where he was going.

Dr. Chambers had been a concert pianist, lived through polio, was very short and my dad treated her like his mother (only better). She would come over to our house and the two of them would play Wagner music very, very loud and discuss classical music. After my parents passed I saved a picture of her and keep it on my desk at home. I have attached it to this letter. You will see why she scared me to death. Maybe she and my dad both helped me get "white coat hypertension."

I was visiting a client at Camden Pet Hospital and your name came up. She mentioned that you saw her at the hospital several years after you had treated her. You came over to her and asked how her headaches were doing. She couldn't believe that you remembered her and expressed how much she appreciated the interest and care she had received. Thank you again for your interest in me and your efforts in trying to help me continue enjoying my wonderful days in the neighborhood.

No One Likes A Frowning Face

I n the late '50s and at least into the '60s my mother was
a chorister for the Sunday School children from the
ages of three to twelve who attended a meeting called
Primary. There are many songs she taught us that I can still
remember ('Jesus Wants me for a Sunbeam', 'Give Said the
Little Stream', 'Popcorn Popping . . . on the apricot tree',
'Father, I Will Reverent Be', 'I Have Two Little Hands',
and a few others). The song that has had the most influence
on my life was one called 'Smiles'. Mother drew a person's
smiley face that if turned upside down would become a
frowny face. She would hold up the frowny face and have
the children sing the lyrics, "If you chance to meet a frown
do not let it stay—Quickly turn it upside down and smile
that frown away". She would turn the drawing to the smiley
side up as they sang the verses to the song. They would then
sing the second verse, "No one likes a frowning face, change
it for a smile—Make the world a better place by smiling
all the while."

Several years ago as my brother, sisters, and I were
going through our parent's belongings we found the smiley

face drawn by mom. I was allowed to keep it and to me it is priceless. Over the years the 'Smiles' song has passed through my mind and lips countless times as I have gone through the ups and downs of life.

"Most of us would agree with the lyrics of the well-known song, "When you're smiling, the whole world smiles with you." But did you know that smiling may also be good for your health? Researchers are finding that smiling slows down the heart rate, reduces stress, and can make you feel happier. In fact, some research suggests that the smile doesn't even have to be genuine—even a forced smile can have a positive effect on your well-being. When you smile, you just feel better. Of course, on long, hard days it can be difficult to summon a smile or muster a grin. But that may be when a smile is needed the most."

James Allen counseled, . . . At the bidding of unlawful thoughts, the body sinks rapidly into disease and decay; at the command of glad and beautiful thoughts, it becomes clothed with youthfulness and beauty . . . Strong, pure, and happy thoughts build up the body in vigor and grace. The body is a delicate and plastic instrument, which responds readily to the thoughts by which it is impressed, and habits of thought will produce their own effects, good or bad, upon it. Out of a clean heart comes a clean life and a clean body . . . If you would perfect your body, guard your mind. If you would renew your body, beautify your mind . . . A sour face does not come by chance; it is made by sour thoughts . . . so a strong body and a bright, happy, or serene countenance can only result from the free admittance into the mind of thoughts of joy and goodwill and serenity . . . With those who have lived righteously, age is calm, peaceful, and softly mellowed, like the setting sun. *James Allen, 'As A Man Thinketh', 1903, p 33-36.*

"One dark, snowy winter day, a young man was walking across a deserted university campus on his way to an early-morning class. It was hard to find anything to smile about that cold and windy morning. And then he heard someone singing—loudly! As he got a little closer, he recognized his roommate walking toward him, singing at the top of his lungs, 'Oh, what a beautiful morning! Oh, what a beautiful day!' It's practically impossible to sing those words without a smile. It can't be done. Now, some may say that this young man was silly or deluded, but those who knew him well understood who he really was—optimistic, upbeat, always on the lookout for the positive.

You can't always do much to change circumstances, So smile. Smile because you are alive. Smile because you live in a glorious world. Smile because there are good people around you who could use a smile. Smile because there's always the promise and hope that life will get better. Having the courage and disposition to greet others and yourself with a smile may be just enough to turn the day around." Program #4373, Music and the Spoken word

> *"If you chance to meet a FROWN do not*
> *let is stay—quickly turn it upside down*
> *and SMILE that frown away"*

Revenge of the Rattlesnake

Rattlesnakes are large, venomous cold-blooded snakes that are found throughout North and South America. The greatest concentration of them is in the Southwestern United States and Northern Mexico. Depending on the time of year and temperature they can be found active during night or day and in the late fall and winter they will congregate in the same den and hibernate (brumate). When it's warm enough in the early spring they will emerge from the den, mate, and set out on their own.

They regulate their body temperature by absorbing the environment and the sun's heat and when it's too hot they will be more active at night. They smell through their nostrils and flicking their tongue in the air, to find pray they have heat radiation sensors in their head, hear mostly by sensing the vibrations from movement in the area, and can't see sharply defined objects around them. They warn intruders by making noise from shaking a rattle, made from a material that resembles a fingernail, at the end of their tail, and will hiss like a cat. If their personal space is disturbed they may strike in defense and deliver venom through two needle-sharp fangs. The young rattlers and those that can't make noise or see when molting their skin are the most aggressive.

There are many old tales or truths about rattlesnakes. It is said that a snake dies after sunset if you cut off its head and that the head should be buried deep or it can still bite. Snakes do continue to have the biting instinct after the head is cut off. It has been known to deliver venom and the body of the snake continues to move for several hours because being cold-blooded the muscles use oxygen more slowly and movement reflexes continue. When sleeping out where snakes are it is said that if you place a horsehair rope around you that a rattlesnake will not cross over the rope. This is debated but it makes sense to me. If the snake smells horse I can reason that it may not cross over the rope. In the old western movies, many a cowboy has awakened with a coiled rattler sitting on his chest or tucked away in his bedroll. I found references that this is true but no references that a drawn gun was used to shot the head off—as seen in the movies.

As a young teenager staying with my family in a cabin near a creek that feeds the middle fork of the Salmon River I remember early one morning with fishing gear in toe running over rocks and boulders along the creek. I planned to start fishing near the source of the creek and fish down. Going over one rock I jumped over the top of a rattlesnake warming up for the day. As my feet landed the body's flight or fight response kicked in and reflexed a backward jump over the snake and then a jump into the creek before I realized what had happened. My fear level was high with thoughts about rattlesnakes traveling in pairs, which I understand is not true, and the just learned truth that a snake can't strike if it is not coiled up.

I worked on a farm while in high school and part of my chores was going out to the fields at daybreak and moving sprinkler lines. They were 20 foot long, 6-inch diameter sections of aluminum pipe and attached in the middle a 2-foot length of 5/8th inch diameter pipe, called a riser, and a sprinkler head. We would disconnect the pipe, lift one end to drain the water, and then move the pipe across several potato rows to the next watering location. When the pipes were all connected the well pump was turned on and the process was repeated at dusk. I bent down to grab a pipe one morning and a snake was lying along the side of the pipe. I suspect the pipe with water inside was warmer than the rest of the field. With my feet sunk in mud and my hand lifting the pipe I was able to get out of the way before the snake could move. So, I know that when a snake is cold it moves slow. I also saw a young rattlesnake whose body was caught under a tractor tire and I know they can strike hard and very rapidly. Reading a book called Arizona's Deadliest Gunfight I also know that rattlesnakes in cold climates often accumulate in large numbers in dens for the winter. I quote, "When the Power family first arrived, rattlesnakes caused such heavy losses among their cattle that the men were forced to locate their den and gas them." I also know that rattlesnakes want to be left alone, won't seek out trouble and their favorite foods are small rodents and lizards. They lie in wait until a victim comes along, and then strike at speeds of five tenths of a second. Their venom paralyzes the prey, which they then swallow whole.

Bishop H. Burke Peterson relates this story, "For much of our lives, we lived in central Arizona. Some years ago a group of teenagers from the local high school went on an all-day picnic into the desert on the outskirts of Phoenix. As some of you know, the desert foliage is rather a sparse mostly mesquite, catclaw, and palo verde trees, with a few cacti scattered here and there. In the heat of the summer, where there are thickets of this desert growth, you may also find rattlesnakes as unwelcome residents. These young people were picnicking and playing, and during their frolicking, one of the girls was bitten on the ankle by a rattlesnake. As is the case with such a bite, the rattler's fangs released venom almost immediately into her bloodstream. This very moment was a time of critical decision. They could immediately begin to extract the poison from her leg, or they could search out the snake and destroy it. Their decision was made, the girl and her young friends pursued the snake. It slipped quickly into the undergrowth and avoided them for fifteen or twenty minutes. Finally, they found it, and rocks and stones soon avenged the infliction.

Then they remembered: their friend had been bitten! They became aware of her discomfort, as by now the venom had had time to move from the surface of the skin deep into the tissues of her foot and leg. Within another thirty minutes, they were at the emergency room of the hospital. By then, the venom was well into its work of destruction.

A couple of days later I was informed of the incident and was asked by some young members of the Church to visit their friend in the hospital. As I entered her room, I saw a pathetic sight. Her foot and leg were elevated-swollen almost beyond recognition. The tissue in her limb had been destroyed by the poison, and a few days later it was found her leg would have to be amputated below the knee. It was a senseless sacrifice, this price of revenge. How much better it would have been if, after the young woman had been bitten, there had been the extraction of the venom from the leg in a process known to all desert dwellers . . ."

There are those today who have been bitten—or offended if you will—by others. What can be done? What will you do when hurt by another? The safe way, the sure way, the right way is to look inward and immediately start the cleansing process. The wise and the happy person removes first the impurities from within. The longer the poison of resentment and unforgiveness stays in a body, the greater and longer-lasting is its destructive effect. As long as we blame others for our condition or circumstance and build a wall of self-justification around ourselves, our strength will diminish, and our power and ability to rise above our situation will fade away. The poison of revenge, or unforgiving thoughts or attitudes, unless removed, will destroy the soul in which it is harbored. *In Conference Report, Oct. 1983, pp. 83-84; or Ensign, Nov. 1983, p. 59.*

I once had an employee, Carol Katzenmeyer, from Camden Pet Hospital call me with an emergency. Her son had been at Calero Dam near San Jose and caught a rattlesnake.

Firmly grabbing it around the neck he got on his bike and rode home with the snake. The final solution was for her son to carefully drop the snake into a container and bring it to the hospital. We placed it in a freezer until it could be properly handled. I don't think her son had any intentions of injuring the rattlesnake and there was a much greater risk of seriously injuring himself—but I think this quote summarizes the potential ending to this story very well.

"No man did a designed injury to another, but at the same time he did a greater to himself." *In The New Dictionary of Thoughts, n. p., p. 309*

The Saga of the M&M's with Peanuts

Traveling by air my wife Shauna and I opened a can't resist Share Size M&M's Peanut package we had purchased just before boarding the plane. I dispensed two of the candies and they were both the same color. We ate them and I dispensed two more. You guessed it, they were the same color—so the game began and ended with two candies of the same color dropping each time out of the small hole in the package until there was the only one left and of course it was also only one color. What a low probability that this event would ever occur and except for my wife, who would ever believe such an event occurred? I felt much like the minister of the Gospel who the story is told loved golf and passed a course every Sunday on his way to church. Oh, how much he wanted to grab his clubs from the trunk of his car and spend a few moments "hitting some balls." One Sunday temptation overruled, he stopped and did something he had never done before—he took a shot from the teeing ground and hit a hole in one. Unless you are a golfer it would be hard to imagine the thrill this gave him and also the disappointment that followed. Being a beautiful Sabbath morning and a man of the cloth who could he tell?

At the heart of every M&M candy is its chocolate, and chocolate has a long history. The cocoa tree is a native plant of South America's river valleys. It was brought north to Mexico by the seventh century A.D. The Mayans and Aztecs made a drink from the beans of the cocoa tree. In 1528, the drink was brought back to Europe by Spanish explorers returning from the New World. The natives blended the cocoa beans with other ingredients including sugar, cinnamon cloves, anise, almonds, hazelnuts, vanilla, and orange-flowered water. It was not until 1828 that a method was developed to produce the solid chocolate that we know today. A Dutch chocolate maker invented a screw press that separated cocoa powder from cocoa butter. Within 20 years, an English company introduced the first commercially successful product. In 1876, Swiss candy makers used dried milk to make solid milk chocolate. In 1904 Hershey Foods marketed one of the first chocolate bars that were both widely affordable and available. In 1913, another Swiss candymaker developed a technique for making chocolate shells filled with other confections. In 1940, Forrest Mars, Sr., and an associate whose name has been lost to history started to manufacture M&Ms'. The M in M&Ms comes from the first initial of the last names of Mars and his associate. And the peanut-centered M&M's were first introduced in 1954.

While doing laundry in a shared home my wife noticed a Peanut M&M's Share Size candy in the refrigerator. We pretty much share everything in our kitchens, pantry, and other areas of the house and she didn't think she would offend anyone by taking the M&M's. It turned out that the M&M's were my daughter-in-law's hidden stash from her kids. Looking for the candy she approached my wife and was given back the candy. When I found out about the incident in a nonconfrontational tone I wrote an apology for the incident explaining why my wife felt comfortable taking the M&M's, how she felt remorse and guilt and left a larger bag of M&M's along with the letter in the refrigerator. The incident was smoothed over and the event was mostly forgotten.

Thomas B. Marsh (1779–1868) was a most capable leader and an apostle in his church in 1835. During this time he and his wife, Elizabeth, lived in Far West Missouri and Mrs. Marsh had made arrangements with George Harris's wife to exchange milk, to make a little more cheese than they otherwise could. To be sure to have justice done, it was agreed that they should not save the strippings (the richest part of the milk), but that the milk and strippings should all go together. Small matters to talk about here, to be sure, two women's exchanging milk to make cheese. When milking cows by hand at the end of milking if the residual milk (called strippings) is removed from the nipple it contains fat percentages that normally is 10%. Raw milk contains about 4.4 % milkfat. "Mrs. Harris, it appeared, was faithful to the agreement and carried to Mrs. Marsh the milk and the strippings, but Mrs. Marsh, wishing to make some extra good cheese, saved a pint of the strippings from each cow and sent Mrs. Harris the milk without the strippings.

"Finally, it leaked out that Mrs. Marsh had saved strippings, and it became a matter to be settled at first between the families, then the church government in which Mr. Marsh was an apostle, and finally after this little affair had kicked up such a breeze in the community and Mrs. Marsh was being found to be in the wrong, Mr. Marsh declared that he would sustain the character of his wife, even if he had to go to hell for it. "In his anger, Thomas B. Marsh then went to the magistrate and swore that the 'Mormons' were hostile to the state of Missouri. This affidavit brought from the government of Missouri an exterminating order, which drove some 15,000 church members from their homes and habitations, and some thousands perished through suffering the exposure consequent on this state of affairs." After 19 years of rancor and loss, Thomas B. Marsh made his way to the Salt Lake Valley and asked President Brigham Young for forgiveness. Brother Marsh also wrote to Heber C. Kimball, First Counselor in the First Presidency, of the lesson he had learned. Said Brother Marsh: "The Lord could get along very well without me and He . . . lost nothing by my falling out of the ranks; But O what have I lost?! Riches, greater riches than all this world or many planets like this could afford." *In Journal of Discourses, 3:283-84.*

Thomas S. Monson wrote, "Many years ago I read the following Associated Press dispatch which appeared in the newspaper: An elderly man disclosed at the funeral of his brother, with whom he had shared, from early manhood, a small, one-room cabin near Canisteo, New York, that following a quarrel, they had divided the room in half with a chalk line, and neither had crossed the line or spoken a word to the other since that day—62 years before. Just think of the consequence of that anger. What a tragedy!"

I know a family through my practice that was contending a piece of property with their siblings left in an estate. What started it was pettiness and the property over the years was becoming of less value from litigation costs alone. This event as well as the M&M's, Thomas Marsh, and the two brothers drawing a chalk line for 62 years over a disagreement were all started from disagreements that could have easily been a so what if nipped in the bud. I don't know the particulars about the property or brother's disagreements but I do know: 1- It is important to recognize that milk fat retained or left in the udder is not lost but will be obtained at succeeding milkings. Although management factors (eg. varying milking intervals and milking frequency) may alter the fat content of milk at one milking, the average fat content over a period of time will be unaffected. With this thought in mind, it appears that Thomas Marsh lost his soul over little of nothing. 2- I found the M&M's empty wrapper by my swimming pool and threw it in the trash, after garbage pickup I found the empty wrapper on the hillside where the trash was picked up, and I placed it again in the garbage can the next week and found again the empty candy wrapper. Therefore, I have taken this highly unusual series of events as an omen of how easily a situation in our family could cause a split family over such a petty event, and as a reminder, I took a picture of the wrapper and placed it in a special place.

School thy feelings, O my brother; train thy warm, impulsive soul. Do not its emotions smother, but let wisdom's voice control. School thy feelings; there is power in the cool, collected mind. Passion shatters reason's tower, Makes the clearest vision blind. *Elder Charles W. Penrose (1832-1925), Hymn—School Thy Feelings.*

"We're Go' in to the Mall"

A t the Hilton in a large room.—Don't have to be gone until about noon.

Here it is about a quarter to seven.—This guy feels like he has been placed in Heaven.

Cause in the bed next to him is his beauty sleeping and facing his way.—

And he's a think' in like only a man can, there's plenty of time for a little more play.

Then he lightly touches her shoulder and whispers a soft expression of love.—

She slowly opens her eyes looking at the clock and makes cooing sounds resembling a dove. With that heart-melting twinkle in her eye and a smile.—

She says, "sweetheart—let's quickly shower, eat, check out of this hotel and hurry to that mall that's less than a mile."

Then he felt vibrations coming up from his feet,— Thinking going to the mall how cool and how neat. And a musical beat flashed into his mind with a descriptive word.—

He suddenly realized they're going to the mall—even with me who's really a nerd.

The words and the music sounded just like this.—And he sang them joyously not a word to miss.

"Guess what! We're going to the mall. Yes, Shauna and Rich are going to the mall.—Shauna and Rich are going to the mall.—Guess what! We're going to the mall.

We're going to have a ball. We're going to the mall.— We're going to the mall. Yes, Shauna and Rich are going to have a ball.

It's just around the corner that way.—Shauna and Rich are getting ready to play We're almost to the mall.—We're going to have a ball, Shauna and Rich are going to the mall.

Oh, ye! We've arrived at the mall.—Yes, Shauna and Rich have arrived at the mall. We're going to have a ball.— Shauna and Rich have arrived at the mall.

Finally, it's closed and we're done at the mall.—Yes, Shauna and Rich are finally done at the mall. We've had a ball.—Shauna and Rich have been at the mall.

Hey man—surprise, we had fun at the mall.—Yes, Shauna and Rich had fun at the mall.

We've really had a ball.—Yes, Shauna and Rich loved going to the mall.

We recommend that all couples should go to the mall.

—Yes, Shauna and Rich recommend that all couples should go to the mall.

We really became close and had a ball. -Shauna and Rich together became close and had a ball at the mall.

Shauna and Rich have been to the mall.—Yes, Shauna and Rich have been to the mall.—Shauna and Rich have had a ball.—Yes, Shauna and Rich have been to the mall and had a ball." Walter R. Hoge, 11/13/2005, written for his wife

Pigeon Racing

Pigeon racing is the sport of releasing specially trained pigeons, which then return to their homes over a carefully measured distance. The time it takes the animal to cover the specified distance is measured and the bird's rate of travel is calculated and compared with all of the other pigeons in the race to determine which animal returned at the highest speed. Training homing pigeons require planned young bird flights progressively farther from the coop and the use of a term called "widowhood." It is usually begun by first allowing the racer to raise a baby in their nest box. After the baby is weaned the hen is removed and often the nest box is closed off. From then on the only time these birds are allowed to see their mate or enter the nest box is upon returning from training or a race. This conditioning is one of the key elements in most racing programs. Pigeon racing, also called Pigeon Flying, uses a specialized variety pigeon, called a Racing Homer, developed through selective crossbreeding for maximum distance and speed in directed flight.

Part of the "animal zoo" I created as a young child, much to the disgust of my father, contained pigeons. He was an MD with a Master's Degree in bacteriology and to him, he saw the destruction of my health and happiness from all the bacteria and parasites these glorified reptiles with feathers could bring into my life. Need I say he was wrong. To me, my father was wrong about most things until I developed some maturity and common sense. To me, dad became a lot smarter and with my maturity, I became less sure of myself.

The earliest record of the domestication of pigeons is from the fifth Egyptian dynasty (about 3000 BC). The sultan of Baghdad established a pigeon post system in AD 1150, and Genghis Khan used such a system as his conquests spread. Pigeons were used as emergency message carriers in war well into the 20th century. The record flight for a U.S. Army Signal Corps pigeon was a flight of 2,300 miles (3,700 km). Flights of 1,000 miles (1,600 km) were routine.

A famous war pigeon named Kaiser's story begins in Koblenz, Germany, in the first week of February 1917. There, in Hans Zimmerman's loft, a young pigeon (or "squeaker") hatched. When he was just five days old, a small aluminum identification band was placed on his left leg, bearing the Imperial German crown. In the Great War, pigeons proved essential in trench warfare. Missed artillery fire caused more casualties than any other weapon, and communication between the forces in the trenches and those in the rear areas was essential to avoid friendly casualties. Artillery fire could cut communication wires and prevent human runners from bringing messages to the rear echelons, but homing pigeons were a low-technology solution, operating swiftly despite bombardments, dust, smoke, and bad weather.

After months of training as a homing pigeon, the bird that would one day be known as "Kaiser" entered frontline service and began flying messages for Kaiser Wilhelm II's German troops in Northern France. In April 1917, just as Kaiser entered the German Army, the United States declared war on Germany. During the fighting in October, American troops captured German prisoners and equipment—including pigeons. Men of the 28th Infantry Division, fighting in the Argonne Forest, captured a German trench line. Among the enemy equipment, the Americans seized was a German pigeon basket with 10 pigeons, including young Kaiser.

When the war ended less than a month later on November 11, 1918, Kaiser remained confined to a pigeon loft with his captured colleagues, his fate undetermined. In December, the Signal Corps decided to bring home distinguished American pigeons together with captured German birds for public relations and morale purposes. On July 17, 1919, Kaiser and 21 other captured German birds arrived in the United States. Once in America, Kaiser was paraded with other captured birds and used for recruiting purposes. Recruiting military trucks displayed Kaiser and other captured pigeons with signs reading, "Captured Germany war prisoners" and "Learn to Fly—PIGEON

SECTION SIGNAL CORPS (Pigeons)—USA." After American entry into World War II, Kaiser's offspring headed to war in Europe and the Pacific, while their father moved to Camp Crowder, Missouri, home to the U.S. Army's Pigeon Breeding and Training Center. By 1945, Kaiser had sired over 75 birds for the army, living in his special white loft with his latest mate, Lady Belle. Moving to Los Angeles, California he was given membership in the American Legion's First Retread Post No. 667, received a gold identification band on his right leg saying "Kaiser—1st Retread 667", and was where he died at the age of 32. *America's Kaiser: How a pigeon served in two World Wars. By Frank Blazich, February 11, 2019.*

Thomas S. Monson relates a story of how an advisor in his priesthood quorum helped teach him while a young teenager the importance of one. "Not long after my ordination as a teacher in the Aaronic Priesthood, I was called to serve as president of the quorum. Our adviser, Harold, was interested in us, and we knew it. One day he said to me, "Tom, you enjoy raising pigeons, don't you?" I responded with a warm, "Yes." Then he proffered, "How would you like me to give you a pair of purebred Birmingham Roller pigeons?" This time I answered, "Yes, Sir!" You see, the pigeons I had were just the common variety, trapped on the roof of the Grant Elementary School. He invited me to come to his home the next evening. The following day was one of the longest in my young life. I was awaiting my adviser's return from work an hour before he arrived home. He took me to his pigeon loft, which was in the upper area of a small barn located at the rear of his yard.

As I looked at the most beautiful pigeons I had yet seen, he said, "Select any male, and I will give you a female which is different from any other pigeon in the world." I made my selection. He then placed in my hand a tiny hen pigeon. I asked what made her so different. He responded, "Look carefully, and you'll notice that she has but one eye." Sure enough, one eye was missing, a cat had done the damage. "Take them home to your loft," he counseled. "Keep them in for about 10 days, and then turn them out to see if they will remain at your place."

I followed Harold's instructions. Upon his release, the male pigeon strutted about the roof of the loft, then returned inside to eat. But the one-eyed female was gone in an instant. I called Harold and asked, "Did that oneeyed pigeon return to your loft?" "Come on over," he said, "and we'll have a look." As we walked from his kitchen door to the loft, my adviser commented, "Tom, you are the president of the teacher's quorum." This, of course, I already knew. Then he added, "What are you going to do to activate Bob, who is a member of your quorum?" I answered, "I'll have him at the quorum meeting this week." Then he reached up to a special nest and handed me the one-eyed pigeon. "Keep her in a few more days and try again." This I did, and once more she disappeared. Again, the experience: "Come on over, and we'll see if she returned home." Came to the comment as we walked to the loft: "Congratulations on getting Bob to priesthood meeting. Now, what are you and Bob going to do to activate Bill?" "We'll have him there next week," I volunteered.

This experience was repeated over and over again. I was a grown man before I fully realized that indeed Harold, my adviser, had given me a special pigeon, the only pigeon in his loft he knew would return every time she was released. It was his inspired way of having an ideal personal priesthood interview with the president of the teacher's quorum every two weeks. I owe a lot to that one-eyed pigeon. I owe more to that quorum adviser. He had the patience and the skill to help me prepare for the responsibilities that lay ahead. *Anxiously Engaged, Thomas S. Monson, General Conference Oct 2004.*

Dr. Jack Hylton and Dr. Patrick Baymiller co-owned Camden Pet Hospital when I began work there. They both raised and raced Racing Homer pigeons. Jack lived close to me and each year when I discussed veterinary medicine with the middle school kiddos I would take some of his pigeons with me. For a final event, the class would go outside to the soccer field and I would discuss racing pigeons and their homing instincts. We each pointed where we thought Dr. Hylton lived and the students would help me release the pigeons. They would circle several times and then head directly to his home on the hill.

Dr. Baymiller had a large loft (dovecot) in the back of his hospital. He raised and raced pigeons many years from his Central Animal Hospital location. After his passing, the loft was eventually torn down. Within the loft, Patrick had been hiding gold coins that rained down during the demolition. No one will ever know if he was hiding his winnings or keeping the gold from his wife.

How carrier pigeons find their way home is still a mystery. According to an article in 2013 scientists have a pretty good idea that pigeons use a magnetic compass guidance system to find general areas near their loft, they may use smell when close to home and they now think pigeons can detect sound waves, called infrasound, that have frequencies well below the range audible to people. "Their using these sounds to image the terrain (surrounding) their loft. It's like us visually recognizing our house using our eyes." Time will hopefully tell the final answers to this question. However, there are times and places when this infrasound will be interrupted or giving false signals that cause pigeons to lose their way. New Theory on How Homing Pigeons Find Home, The birds could be using the specific sound signatures of home to navigate. *By Jane J. Lee, National Geographic News, 01- 30-2013.*

As a boy working on maturity, I was kind of like that the one-eyed racing pigeon. I didn't have a grasp on the forces pulling at me that could hinder or help me get home. But I knew, like the "widowhood" pigeons, that I would be safe at my mother's loft and hopefully feel that way at my future loft and be comfortable being accepted at the loft prepared for all of us as we leave planet earth.

During my mother's life when I lived away, I would at times find my way back to my mother's loft. It was always good to be home to roost, there was warmth and love in the coop, she was there to listen to my ups and downs, and most of all she always had a smile on her face.

My most cherished memories were when in my older years I returned to my mom's coop, sat down at her table, and she would stand behind me, put her hands on my shoulders and say, "How's my little Richie Boy?"

Life As It Is

American illustrator Norman Rockwell is known throughout the world for his optimistic and affectionate portraits of life. His world on canvas depicts real people—friends, neighbors, and family—doing real things. During his 84 years, he painted over 300 covers for the Saturday Evening Post. And, while critics were often not kind, most people were instinctively drawn to his art. Somehow it reminded them of the goodness in life. As Rockwell once noted, "I paint life as I would like it to be."

Arthur C. Brooks, a contributing writer at The Atlantic wrote, "I have seen these paintings my whole life, starting with my grandfather's beloved, dog-eared coffee-table book of Rockwell's greatest works. A printing-press operator in Longview, Washington, my grandfather was no art connoisseur. But he gave this assessment of Rockwell: 'These pictures make me feel happy.' And yet, Rockwell himself struggled with happiness. In 1953, he moved to Stockbridge, Massachusetts, a bucolic town in the Berkshires—not for its natural beauty and peace but because it happened to be the home of a psychiatric hospital where he and his wife could receive treatment for chronic depression. There, he was a patient of the world famous psychoanalyst Erik Erikson, with whom Rockwell racked up a therapy bill so large that he had to accept commissions for Kellogg's Corn Flakes magazine ads."

Two years after my father the M.D. retired he told me, "I treated depression all my medical career and didn't really know what it was until I retired." Unfortunately, severe forms of depression all too often can occur in the field of veterinary medicine. *In 2018 Mental Health/ Psychology magazine* specifically cited depression and potential suicide among veterinarians are attributed to, "long work hours, work overload, practice management responsibilities, client expectations and complaints, euthanasia procedures, and poor work-life balance. Studies have also shown that anxiety and depression are common among veterinarians, as are related personality traits such as perfectionism." There are more applications for available classroom spots in veterinary medicine than for those applying for medical school. Therefore, most students are used to being competitive, high achievers and are not prepared for the failures one needs to expect when working with a living organism. During my career, I have found that preparing myself as best I can for every needful thing, understanding the reality that there are times when the what if's will raise their ugly heads, explaining the proposed therapy in a way that the patient's owner can understand and giving them at least three options on how we can proceed lowers my anxiety level, helps me not be over depressed and reduces self-chastisement when unexpected results come my way. Knowing as best we can the risks and benefits of the procedure in question, the owner needs to make the final decision. The choices usually are: Will we proceed as discussed, try other medications or treatments that may help relieve discomfort but have less of a chance to cure the condition, or doing nothing and waiting and watching to see how the pet will do.

Rockwell could have easily painted, as some say, "life as it is." He could have concentrated on scenes of his or others sorrow and moments of misery. He might have painted the mean and nasty, the cruel and depraved. His canvas could have been colored with conflict and despair. Certainly, such hopeless hues could be found—both then and now. Painting his way through his mental health problems, the Depression, and two world wars, he did not live in a trouble-free world, to be sure! And yet, Rockwell chose to look for the good, the kind, the simple and happy moments that make life worth living.

Think what would happen if we were to choose to paint like Rockwell did—in our mind's eye—life as we would like it to be. We might find more love, more friendship, more forgiveness—because we are looking for it. Perhaps we would appreciate more of the simple pleasures, small gestures, and gentle remarks that are directed our way. Maybe the horizon would not seem so ominous, streets so dangerous, hearts so cold. Maybe if staff members in veterinary facilities would paint their lives as the chronically depressed Norman Rockwell and his wife did it would help keep in perspective the entrustment pet owners have given us to contribute to the health and wellbeing of the one that greets them at the door each time they enter their home and helps give the owner joy and purpose in life. My sub-conscience mindset is to try to think like an animal. No matter what comes their way our pets, or for that matter any member of the animal or plant kingdom, adjusts or dies. They can show a sense of loss, but don't fear death, and even when things are not going good for them they seem to make the best of it and don't have a depressing or bad day. That's good for them and makes for very good days in my work environment.

To those who argue that this "rose-colored" view of the world is not realistic, we acknowledge the ugly side of life. But beautiful things happen on ugly days, and joy can be discovered amidst the sadness of life. Referring to Norman Rockwell, one art critic wrote, "He . . . reassured (people) of their essential goodness. And that is a very powerful thing." So powerful that, for many of us, Rockwell's "life as he would like it to be" is somehow remembered as life as it was: the "good old days" for which we may long. Believe it, I have had very close touching experiences with clients that are attending the euthanasia of their pet. Younger clients seem to be more down or depressed and show more of the emotions one would expect during a personal or family crisis. Elderly clients usually live alone, with a spouse or family, or in a care facility. They generally do not show outward emotions—they seem to have accepted the circle of life and do not want their dear pet/ companion to continue to suffer whether it be physical and/or cognitive loss of function. Most are having more difficult than good days and seem to be more comfortable with their and their pet's fate. They express in one way or the other that they are recognizing their friends aging changes and are unselfishly not wanting them to suffer. If the moment seems right, I often mention while performing euthanasia that I had watched the mood of my father, a smalltown M.D., many times when he was caring for a terminally ill patient. Especially those who he had grown up with and/or were personal friends. Watching my father's struggles early in my life helped me chose a career where there did not need to be such suffering.

One evening our family was having dinner and I overheard my father say on the phone, "Go ahead and kill yourself. I could care less!" A doctor saying this to a patient seemed malicious and a malpractice statement to me. The next evening my courage allowed me to ask dad what happened. With a smile, he said that he knew she would not kill herself. He had intentionally angered her enough that she was not going to kill herself until she had a chance to let dad know how angry she was about the way he had treated her. Let us remember, those good old days are never over. We, too, can paint life as we'd like it to be. And the more we look, the more good we will find, and the more "life as we would like it to be" will become life as it is. And that's a very powerful thing. Portions were from, *Lloyd D. Newell, "Life As It Is", Music & The Spoken Word, Oct 17, 1993.*

By deliberately preparing yourself to cheer up the people around you the way a happy person spontaneously would, you'll create the conditions by which you can produce your happiness naturally—and give the gift of happiness to others, as well. *"How to Build a Life" is a weekly column by Arthur Brooks, tackling questions of meaning and happiness.*

Letter to The New Owners
Serenity Way, San Jose

Forty years ago this last spring (1976) my children's mom sat on a couch in the front room of this house. I had recently accepted a position as a veterinarian in the area and we were looking for a home. My wife was carrying in her arms a ten-month-old son, we were in the process of adopting, and another one in her womb that would be born approximately two weeks later. She told me that, "she was exhausted and could go no further. This home would be the right place for us to raise our family".

Not long after we moved in, my employer, Dr. Hylton, dropped by the home and asked to take a look. As he walked through each room in the house he kept saying, "it's a crying shame" and then walked out of the house and headed for his car. I followed him to the street curb and asked, "What is a crying shame?" I was concerned that we had moved into a bad neighborhood, the home was in a high-risk earthquake zone, the schools were bad, it was built by a questionable contractor etcetera. He looked me straight in the eye and told me it was a crying shame what my children would do to this home as they were growing up.

We raised five children in your new home and they did make their mark—to me these marks have become precious memories. They have all gotten a good education, all but one is married and they are doing a great job raising my 15 grandchildren. I think you will also have good experiences raising your children here and precious memories will follow you for the rest of your lives.

I was preparing this home for my retirement until one of my sons found me a place that would be a little more "user friendly" as age caught up with me. Therefore, I think you will find the home in good condition and problem-free for many years. Below is a list of a few things that I would like to make you aware of: (list deleted)

I hope these thoughts are of some help. It was hard for me to leave the home and all the memories. If one day an older gentleman knocks at your door, maybe he will just want to walk around looking at the rooms and mumbling something like "It's a crying shame." May you have a wonderful life and your family enjoy the best it has to offer . . .

This is Us
Our Life. Our Story. Our Home

Faith of a Father Fareed

In 1979 a close friend of mine, Dale Stewart, along with all the employees of Ford Aerospace suddenly left all their equipment behind and fled Iran. There had just been an uprising of the citizens there that became known as the Iran hostage crisis. It began on November 4, 1979, when a group of Iranian students in Tehran, the capital of Iran, stormed the American embassy. They trapped fifty-two American workers there and held them, hostage, for 444 days. The incident was a dramatic way for the student revolutionaries to declare a break from Iran's past and attempt to put an end to American interference in the region.

I mention this because of several conversations I have had in the past with a client/friend of mine, his conversion to Christianity at 15 years of age, conflict with his father, leaving Iran to live in the United States, and the difficulty doing his work as he spreads the Gospel of Christ throughout the world. First, let me share with you some of the events that influenced his life and choices.

Mohammad Reza Pahlavi, "The Shah of Iran", (26 October 1919–27 July 1980), was the last Shah of Iran from 16 September 1941 until his overthrow by the Iranian Revolution on 11 February 1979. His dream of what he referred to as a «Great Civilization» in Iran led to a rapid industrial and military modernization, as well as economic and social reforms. He also introduced the White Revolution, a series of economic, social, and political reforms with the proclaimed intention of transforming Iran into a global power and modernizing the nation by nationalizing certain industries and granting women suffrage. Mohammad Reza gradually lost support from the Shi'a clergy of Iran as well as the working class, his relations with Israel, corruption issues surrounding himself, his family, and the ruling elite, as well as a general suppression of political dissent, and the US and UK support of his regime.

The Shah was diagnoses with cancer in 1974 and by 1979, political unrest had transformed into a revolution which, on 17 January, forced him to leave Iran. Soon thereafter, the Iranian monarchy was formally abolished, and Iran was declared an Islamic republic led by Ruhollah Khomeini. Facing likely execution should he return to Iran, he died in exile in Egypt.

Recently, in December 2018, my client, Pastor Donald Fareed, visited Camden Pet Hospital to receive care for his pet "Joy." Being the Christmas season, I mentioned his father and how difficult it must have been to leave his father behind in Iran at 22 years of age and not having the important relationships a son would like to have with his father. He told me that was not the whole story and we sat down and had a wonderful visit. I asked Pastor Fareed to share this story about his father. He prefaced his remarks with the statement, "Hello and happy new year. Here is the modified part of your article that is related to my dad. May God bless you for glorifying Christ through this. Don."

"I told Rich that the last time I saw my father was over 25 years ago when he came to the U.S. to visit me and encourage me to stop sharing the Gospel due to the concerns he had for my safety as well as the safety of those related to me who still lived in Iran. Due to my Christian ministry among Iranians as well as my television broadcast I used to receive threats regularly and I had lost beloved friends who had been either jailed or killed for their faith. My popularity had made life difficult for those like my father who had stayed behind in Iran. During his visit, my father also had an encounter with Jesus Christ and converted to Christianity. Instead of staying in the U.S., my father returned to Iran to personally share the Gospel with his own family and friends who had become disillusioned with Islam. Unfortunately, after a few months of being in Iran and sharing the Gospel, at the age of 75 the Sharia court condemned him to receive 80 lashes which caused him to have a brain stroke which he never recovered from. Following this incident, my father was bedridden for 7 years until he finally went home to be with his Lord and Savior. Those who visited him during the last 7 years of his life testified that his faith in Christ grew stronger even after his stroke. Not being able to talk, he always greeted his guests by pointing his finger to the sky and a cross on the wall with enthusiasm, joy, and smile to express his faith in Christ who had saved his soul and life so he could share the Gospel until his last breath. How he handled his pains and suffering as well as the injustice that had been done to him continued to inspire many. Despite the obvious danger in Iran, many of his family members and friends in Iran were inspired to put their faith in Jesus Christ. He finally went to his beloved Lord and Savior in September 2000." www.PersianMinistries.org, https://persianministries.org/about/founder.php.

Like Pastor Don Fareed's family and friends, we all have fears and anxieties. Unlike a lot of us; with all the challenges Pastor Fareed's father had, "he always greeted his guests by pointing his finger to the sky and a cross on the wall with enthusiasm, joy, and smile." You see he was "expressing his faith in Christ who had saved his soul and life so he could share the Gospel until his last breath." It was his testimony that God and His son Jesus Christ loves us—always—and our love of them counters all fears. "Those who visited him during the last 7 years of his life testified that his faith in Christ grew stronger even after his stroke."

Jesus Christ was the Great Jehovah of the Old Testament, the Messiah of the New. Under the direction of His Father, He was the creator of the earth. "All things were made by him, and without him was not anything made that was made" (John 1:3). Though sinless, He was baptized to fulfill all righteousness. He "went about doing good" (Acts 10:38), yet was despised for it. His gospel was a message of peace and goodwill. He entreated all to follow His example. He walked the roads of Palestine, healing the sick, causing the blind to see, and raising the dead. He taught the truths of eternity, the reality of our premortal existence, the purpose of our life on earth, and the potential for the sons and daughters of God in the life to come. He instituted the sacrament as a reminder of His great atoning sacrifice. He was arrested and condemned on spurious charges, to satisfy a mob, and sentenced to die on Calvary's cross. He gave His life to atone for the sins of all mankind. His was a great vicarious gift on behalf of all who would ever live upon the earth. His life, which is central to all human history, neither began in Bethlehem nor concluded on Calvary. He was the Firstborn of the Father, the Only Begotten Son in the flesh, the Redeemer of the world. He rose from the grave to "become the first fruits of them that slept" (1 Corinthians 15:20). As Risen Lord, He visited among those He had loved in life. He also ministered among His "other sheep" (John 10:16) in ancient America.

The Iranian hostages were released on January 20, 1981, the day President Carter's term ended. The Iranians had insisted on payment in 50 tons of gold to Iran while simultaneously taking ownership of an equivalent quantity of Iranian gold that had been frozen at the New York Federal Reserve Bank. Donald Fareed's father was released from his 80 lashes bedridden induced stroke's confinement to return to his Father in Heaven in 2000.

***How he handled his pains and suffering,
as well as the injustice that had been done to him,***

continued to inspire many
—"We can feel God's love & perfect love
casts out all fear . . ." Moroni 8:16

Worry ends
when faith begins

Sugar Beets and Falling of the Truck

U kraine possesses more than ¼ of the world's black soil. The word Chornozem, meaning "black earth" has become internationally recognized and refers to Ukrainian soil, celebrated as the most fertile possible. Byzantine emperor Constantine VII, way back in the 10th century wrote, "The best soil is Chornozem. It is not afraid of rain or drought." Even the French writer Balzak, after visiting Ukraine, praised these lands in his writings. Ukraine's rich soil was probably one of the reasons why the first agricultural civilizations in Europe emerged and developed here in the 5-4th centuries B.C. *Bloomberg Businessweek, 01/08/2018,* stated, "It could be a picture of rural prosperity: Workers steer grumbling trucks and red harvesters as high as houses harvesting sugar beets and churning 1,400 acres of snowy farmland into thick, black mud. The early winter scene, about 250 miles from Kiev, instead illustrates Ukraine's failure to drag its most historically significant industry into the 21st century." Seeing sugar beets harvested in Idaho, I was surprised that such a fertile area of the world had small sugar beets shown in a photo of a harvester. The sugar beets didn't look anything like the 5 to 7-pound beets I would see lying along the side of the road that had fallen from the transport trucks in Idaho.

My wife's brother Tim (he worked for the Amalgamated Sugar Company in Nampa Idaho), during the harvest season, took me for a tour of his sugar company. I was so impressed that I collected sugar beets off the side of the road that had fallen from the harvest trucks and told Tim that I was going to make sugar. He had a good laugh and I flew the beets back with me to San Jose. During Thanksgiving Vacation 2010 my visiting in-laws helped peel, cut up and boil these sugar beets for several days until we gave up making table sugar. We had produced a product that looked like molasses. I placed and sealed the product in darkened glass containers and labeled them: *Idaho beet molasses, From Tim's Road Side Stand, Produced from pure sugar beets, water evaporation, our loving care & $30.00 of California electricity . . ., Green Things To Eat Company, San Jose, CA—A star ***** Brand, 11/22/10.* What I learned from the extraction process was that there is a lot of sweetness in sugar beets that have slipped off the truck and were lying in the gutter.

Thomas S. Monson, July 2009 Ensign, mentioned comments made by Marvin O. Ashton (1883-1946) picturing a farmer driving along a bumpy dirt road with some of the sugar beets in his loaded truck falling along the roadside. When he realized he had lost some of the beets, he instructed his helpers—"There's just as much sugar in those which slipped off. Let's go back and get them!" As we travel down the road in our lives, "There are many of us that have 'slipped off the truck' of life and find ourselves in that dreaded 'Never, Never Land'—never the object of concern, never the recipient of needed aid. It may not be our privilege to open gates of cities or doors of palaces, but true happiness and lasting joy will come to (us) and to each one (we) serve as (we) take a hand and reach (out to) a heart (in need)."

Melinda Gates wrote, Ten years ago, I traveled to India with friends. On the last day there, I spent some time meeting with prostitutes. I expected to talk to them about the risk of AIDS, but they wanted to talk about stigma. Most of these women had been abandoned by their husbands, and that's why they'd gone into prostitution. They were trying to make enough money to feed their kids. They were so low in the eyes of a society that they could be raped and robbed and beaten by anybody-even by police-and nobody cared. Talking to them about their lives was so moving to me. But, what I remember most is how much they wanted to touch me and be touched. It was as if physical contact somehow proved their worth. As I was leaving, we took a photo of all of us with our arms linked together.

Later that day I spent some time in a home for the dying. I walked into a large hall and saw rows and rows of cots. Every cot was attended except for one far off in the corner that no one was going near, so I walked over there. The patient was a woman who seemed to be in her thirties. I remember her eyes. She had these huge, brown, sorrowful eyes. She was emaciated, on the verge of death. Her intestines weren't holding anything-so they had put her on a cot with a hole cut out in the bottom, and everything just poured through into a pan below. I could tell she had AIDS, both from the way she looked, and the fact that she was off in the corner alone. The stigma of AIDS is vicious-especially for women-and the punishment is abandonment. When I arrived at her cot, I suddenly felt totally helpless. I had absolutely nothing I could offer her. I knew I couldn't save her, but I didn't want her to be alone. So, I knelt next to her and reached out to touch her-and as soon as she felt my hand, she grabbed it and wouldn't let go. We sat there holding hands, and even though I knew she couldn't understand me, I just started saying: "It's okay, it's okay. It's not your fault. It's not your fault." We had been there together for a while when she pointed upward with her finger.

It took me some time to figure out that she wanted to go up to the roof and sit outside while it was still light out. I asked one of the workers if that would be okay, but she was overwhelmed by all the patients she had to care for. She said: "She's in the last stages of dying, and I have to pass out medicine." Then I asked another and got the same answer. It was getting late and the sun was going down, and I had to leave, and no one seemed willing to take her upstairs. So finally, I just scooped her up-she was just skin over a skeleton, just a sack of bones-and I carried her up the stairs. On the roof, there were a few of those plastic chairs that will blow over in a strong breeze, and I set her down on one of those, and I helped prop her feet up on another, and I placed a blanket over her legs. And, she sat there with her face to the west, watching the sunset. I made sure the workers knew that she was up there so they would come to get her after the sun went down. Then, I had to leave her. But, she never left me. I felt completely and totally inadequate in the face of this woman's death. But, sometimes it's the people you can't help who inspire you the most. I knew that the sex workers I linked arms with in the morning could become the woman I carried upstairs in the evening-unless they found a way to defy the stigma that hung over their lives.

Over the past 10 years, our foundation has helped sex workers build support groups so they could empower each other to speak out for safe sex and demand that their clients use condoms. Their brave efforts helped keep HIV prevalence low among sex workers, and a lot of studies show that is a big reason why the AIDS epidemic in India hasn't exploded. When these sex workers gathered together to help stop AIDS transmission, something unexpected and wonderful happened. The community they formed became a platform for everything. They were able to set up speed-dial networks to respond to violent attacks. Police and others who raped and robbed them couldn't get away with it anymore. The women set up systems to encourage savings. They used financial services that helped some of them start businesses and get out of sex work. This was all done by people society considered the lowliest of the low. Optimism for me isn't a passive expectation that things will get better; it's a conviction that we can make things better-that whatever suffering we see, no matter how bad it is, we can help people if we won't lose hope and we don't look away. *Malinda Gates, The Poser of not Looking Away, Stanford University Graduation, 2014.*

Few things define Ukraine more than farming. Its people have lived, toiled, and starved on the land for centuries, and their economic and political struggles are dug deep into the soil. It's here that Joseph Stalin's forced collectivization drive exacted its heaviest toll. From 6 to 7 million Ukrainians perished in the 1932-33 famine. Many throughout the world have been treated harshly because of personal choices, governments, religion, traditions, or just bad luck. However, no matter how we came to "slip off the truck" or how far we find ourselves in the gutter—there is still potentially as much sugar in us as there is in those still on the truck.

Optimism for me isn't a passive expectation that
things will get better; it's a conviction that we can make
things better—that whatever suffering we see,
no matter how bad it is, we can help people if
we don't lose hope and we don't look away. Malinda Gates

How think ye? If a man have an hundred sheep,
and one of them be gone astray, doth he not leave the
ninety and nine, and goeth into the mountains, and
seeketh that which is gone astray? Matthew 18:12

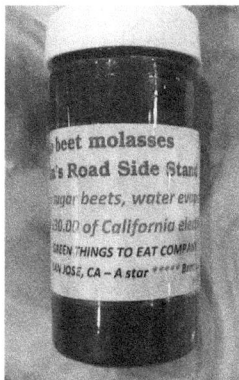

When Warned—Will We Listen?

- News report published on 8:52 AM September 17, 2015:

- The seven victims were visiting the Zion National Park in Utah on Monday

- They were warned in advance of a 40 percent chance of flash flooding

- Park Rangers told the victims that they should not visit the park that day

- The leader of the group had experience exploring the canyon

- All were in their 50's some had taken a canyoneering course

- Keyhole Canyon's route is considered to be entry level—80 permits issued a day

- The park was closed later that day when the weather situation worsened

- One inch of rain fell in less than an hour, swelling the North Fork of the Virgin River, which Keyhole Canyon drains into

- The bodies of all the victims have now been recovered Darren Boyle for MAILONLINE

I was also in my 50's when a call came through from a member of the San Jose Police Department. His name was Mark Conrad and we had worked together over the years in the scouting program. He mentioned that he had two top-notch youth that had graduated from high school and were working some but mostly hanging around waiting to go off to college. As a special treat, Mark wanted to take them along with me to Zion National Park and hike the Zion Narrows on the Virgin River. I told him to give me a day or two to see if I could arrange to be gone from my work and family. I didn't tell him at the time, but I mostly wanted to find out what he was getting me into. He's the type of guy that took the youth to climb Half Dome in Yosemite National Park and bike rides from San Jose to Disney Land.

I found an article that read much like this: "If any place has the power to inspire awe, it's the Zion Narrows, southern Utah's premier hike in Zion National Park. For 16 miles (26 kilometers), the canyon winds voluptuously through the crimson sandstone, in some spots stretching 2,000 feet (610 meters) high and narrowing to 20 feet

(6 meters). Lush hanging gardens spring from the walls, stately ponderosa pines grow in nooks, and the water can turn a shade of turquoise that perfectly contrasts with the cliffs' deep terra-cotta hues. The hike isn't necessarily a cakewalk, however: For more than half the time, hikers walk in the Virgin River, which can be waist-high, and negotiate cobbles as large and slippery as bowling balls." *National Geographic And, Joe's hiking guide* mentions the need for, "permits, preparation for camping overnight, need for water footwear, hiking poles (I still have my walking stick that has Zion National Park burned on it), a dry pack, easy drying clothing, quality backpacking gear, and a headlamp."

With some hesitancy, I soon found myself in a car heading to Utah with Mark Conrad and our two youth (Brandon Crockett and Michael Folk), we slept overnight on the steps where permits were given out on an early morning basis (only a few were given out each day), rented a motel room close to the park and the next morning met some friends that drove us to the entry point on the Virgin River. After checking in and given a weather clearance, off we went hiking into the Zion Narrows water or on cliff trails along the Virgin River.

When I read the report in September 2015 about the loss of hikers much more experienced and capable of taking care of themselves than we were—I appreciated how Mark had been taught to be cautious and to "go by the rules", making it possible for us to have some safe special moments with a couple of sons that belonged to our friends. Sleeping on a sand bar halfway through Zion Narrows reminded me of many years before when my family was sleeping in a small boat on a sand bar at the base of a dam in Arizona. During the middle of the night, they let water out of the dam, and as the water level rose our boat was lifted and rolled onto its side giving all of us a rude awakening. It took a lot of effort to rapidly pull the boat to higher ground. I'm sure you can understand why I had trouble sleeping on that sand bar halfway through the Narrows.

On December 26, 2004, a powerful earthquake struck off the coast of Indonesia, creating a deadly tsunami that killed more than 200,000 people. It was a terrible tragedy. In one day, millions of lives were forever changed. But there was one group of people who, although their village was destroyed, did not suffer a single casualty. The reason? They knew a tsunami was coming. The Moken people live in villages on islands off the coast of Thailand and Burma (Myanmar). A society of fishermen, their lives depend on the sea. For hundreds and perhaps thousands of years, their ancestors have studied the ocean, and they have passed their knowledge down from father to son. One thing, in particular, they were careful to teach was what to do when the ocean receded. According to their traditions, when that happened, the "Laboon"—a wave that eats people—would arrive soon after. When the elders of the village saw the dreaded signs, they shouted to everyone to run to the high ground. Not everyone listened. One elderly fisherman said, "None of the kids believed me." In fact, his own daughter called him a liar. But the old fisherman would not relent until all had left the village and climbed to higher ground.

"Sea Gypsies See Signs in the Waves," CBS News, 60 Minutes transcript, Mar. 20, 2005.

The Moken people were fortunate in that they had someone with conviction who warned them of what would follow. The villagers were fortunate because they listened. Had they not, they may have perished.

I appreciate how Mark was one that had been taught to be cautious and to "go by the rules." Being who I am, I still vividly remember constantly looking for the water to rise as I tried to sleep on a sand bar halfway through the Narrows.

We should never so entirely avoid danger as to appear irresolute and cowardly; but, at the same time, we should avoid unnecessarily exposing ourselves to danger, than which nothing can be more foolish . . .
Cicero, Marcus Tullius 106-43 B.C.

Brother's Day May 24th

Informing me that May 24th was Brothers Day, my dear friend (Ron Reimers) from my childhood texted me this quote: "A real man is the kind of man that when your feet hit the floor each morning the devil says "Oh . . . (darn)! He's up!" Brother, life is too short to wake up with regrets. So, love the people who treat u right. Forgive the ones who don't just because you can. Believe everything happens for a reason. If you get a second chance, grab it with both hands. If it changes your life, let it. Take a few minutes to think before u act when you're mad. Forgive quickly. God never said life would be easy. He just promised it would be worth it. Today is Brother's Day, send this to all your Brothers, Fathers, Sons. Happy Brothers Day! I LOVE YA BROTHER!!! To the cool men that have touched my life. Here's to you!! A real Brother walks with u when the rest of the world walks on you. Send it to all your Brothers because the fake ones won't send it . . . And have a great weekend." *Mark Linton.*

For most of my early life up until about nine years of age, I lived in Blackfoot Idaho within three blocks of the railroad tracks and Main Street. I was told that our Main Street is the widest in the country. That is because there are two Main Streets in Blackfoot. A North West and a North East Main Street. They parallel each other with one on one side of the train tracts and one on the other side of the train tracts. For a town of a few thousand residents, I thought that was pretty cool.

I remember the train tracts because my brother (John) who was six years younger than me would have to be tied into his crib at night or he would wander away from the house, cross the tracks, and often end up in the bars lining Main Street. This was a concern for my brother's health and well-being but also didn't leave a good parenting impression especially since my father was one of the local medical doctors in town.

My friend Ron lived across the street from my house in the American Legion Home. His parents cared for the building and helped with organizational activities. Ron's mother treated me with kindness and respect and we had a blast in the home. I remember playing army with WW I & II guns and target shooting our BB guns at targets in the basement. A favorite target was the string hanging down used to turn on and off the light. There were times the shots strayed a little high and we were in the dark after hitting the light bulb. We stayed good friends right on through high school and applied for the Air Force Academy together. After written exams, we went to Hill Airforce Base in Utah for physicals. Each of us was not offered enrollment at the academy but I'll always remember that trip. While I was in a dental chair word filtered through the building that John F. Kennedy had been assassinated and I'll always remember the mood change on the base.

Ron and I ended up at the University of Idaho. He graduated and went to Viet Nam to fly helicopters and I continued my education at Purdue University. There was little contact until we met with our wives at our 50th high school class reunion. It felt like it was just yesterday since we had seen each other and it led to a couple of cruises together, a stay in San Jose, and a relighting of a glow that has always been between us. Our close friendship led Ron to send me the above quote from Mark Linton.

At the state funeral for former United States President George H. W. Bush in December 2018, former Canadian Prime Minister Brian Mulroney ended the eulogy of his dear friend with these words: "There are wooden ships, there are sailing ships, there are ships that sail the sea. But the best ships are friendships, and may they always be."

How else can we possibly expect to make it across life's rough seas? Friendships make the voyage not only possible but also enjoyable. Among life's richest blessings is friendship. And while the waves and winds may separate good friends for a time—even years—when they reunite, the time and distance fade almost instantly.

Perhaps you've had an experience similar to that of two dear friends who lost contact with each other. Many years and many miles later, one of them remembered and missed their bond of friendship, so he decided to take the initiative to find his friend. After decades apart, the friends reconnected, and the joyous reunion melted the years away. Their hearts filled with happiness and fond memories as they laughed together and shared tender feelings. It was as if they had never parted—as if they still lived in the same town and shared the same experiences.

Most of us can remember friends who have touched our lives for good over the years. Some of those friends may now be gone, but the memory of their love, example, and goodness can still lift and inspire us. The love and trust, the listening and caring, the shared time and experiences never really leave us, because they have made us who we are. Although we may sometimes appear to be independently strong, no one crosses life's waters alone. We need to have— and need to be—true friends. Transcript: Brian Mulroney's Eulogy for Former President George H. W. Bush," CBS News, Dec. 6, 2018 and Music, and the Spoken Word, March 3, 2019, Number 4,668

We often are given the impression that to truly be happy and successful we need to be independently strong and able to travel through life without anyone there to help bear our burdens, or suffer and moan with us during difficult times or comfort us when we need to be comforted. Without having a shoulder to lean on and shed a few tears from time to time we open ourselves to becoming a crotchety, bitter, regretful, and depressed person. Let me share a story (Man Does Not Stand Alone) related by Henry D. Taylor illustrating how we will be much happier in life if we grow together and not separate ourselves from our family or friends:

"A boy was extended an invitation to visit his uncle who was a lumberjack up in the Northwest . . . [As he arrived] his uncle met him at the depot, and as the two pursued their way to the lumber camp, the boy was impressed by the enormous size of the trees on every hand. There was a gigantic tree which he observed standing all alone on the top of a small hill. The boy, full of awe, called out excitedly, 'Uncle George, look at that big tree! It will make a lot of good lumber, won't it?'

"Uncle George slowly shook his head, then replied, 'No, son, that tree will not make a lot of good lumber. It might make a lot of lumber but not a lot of good lumber. When a tree grows off by itself, too many branches grow on it. Those branches produce knots when the tree is cut into lumber. The best lumber comes from trees that grow together in groves. The trees also grow taller and straighter when they grow together.'"

Then Brother Taylor made this observation: "It is so with people. We become better individuals, more useful timber when we grow together rather than alone." *Conference Report, April 1965, pp. 54–55.*

Elder Sterling W. Sill, in an article entitled "Men in Step," wrote: "The greatest invention of all time is said to have taken place 2500 years ago at Platea when an obscure Greek perfected the process of marching men in step. When it was found that the efforts of a large group of people having different motives and different personalities could be organized and coordinated to function as one, that day civilization began." *"Insights & Perspectives,"* March 1977, from Leadership, Bookcraft, 1958, 1:222–29

God never said life would be easy. He just promised it would be worth it. Today is Brother's Day, send this to all your Brothers, Fathers, Sons. Happy Brothers Day!
I LOVE YA BROTHER!!!

Our Elf On The Shelf Nearly Started A Fire

D ear Dad,

Hello! How are you? Things here are going well. We are in the frenzy of all the holiday shopping, planning, activities, etc. the kids are beyond excited—especially Naomi. She couldn't wait to get the tree and decorations up. It was a relief to me when we finally had it done. Now she won't be asking me nonstop to do it! What are your plans for Christmas? Will you be in Idaho?

We had a near holiday catastrophe on Monday afternoon. Our Elf on the Shelf almost caught fire! Do you know about the Elf on the Shelf? It's a ridiculous tradition that every young parent these days makes the mistake of starting to think it will be so cute and fun. They don't realize how much work it is, and that it's not a one-time thing. You have to continue the tradition from year to year even though you get burned out. (I gave one to Jeremy and Heather a few years ago. I feel a little guilty about that now.) the Elf sits in a spot and watches the kids during the day. He has to sit in a high spot to avoid anyone touching him—if he gets touched the magic is lost. Each night he goes to the North Pole to report to Santa if the kids are being naughty or nice. You know he left because he appears each morning in a new spot. This means that each night mom or dad has to remember to move the Elf to a new place. Sometimes you forget and wake in a panic to move it before anyone wakes up. Sometimes you forget completely, and the Elf just doesn't move. Then you have to come up with some story as to why he didn't move and assure everyone that he's okay. It gets exhausting.

Anyway, I foolishly hooked the Elf up on the lightbulb of one of the fans in the bonus room Sunday night. I thought about the bulb being too hot, but then I thought we just wouldn't turn on the light. I was resting on the couch after helping Delaney with her homework. I just couldn't keep my eyes open. Naomi came in at some point and said very calmly, "Mom?" I told her to please let me have a few minutes to rest. She replied, "This is kind of important. I could smell burning and see smoke." I sat right up. I knew exactly what she was talking about. The Elf! Luckily, she was smart and immediately turned the light out. No harm done. Except that the Elf had melted to the light bulb. He lost about a 2-inch section of his arm. The kids were so worried—all 3 of the little ones were there to witness it. Naomi kept telling me not to touch him. She was so worried I would ruin his magic. He was stuck to the light bulb, so I unscrewed it and was able to get him down by just touching the light bulb. Whew! We put him in a box like a wounded bird. Then I told them just to wait and see what happens. I didn't know what happens to injured elves.

How was I going to fix this?! I could just buy a new Elf, but they're expensive and I kind of resent the one we have. Should I just let him "die" and bury this silly tradition? No. I had to fix it. It's too important to the kids. So, I went to the store and found some Elf pajamas. (They sell all kinds of accessories for the Elf on the shelf.) I put them on to cover the destroyed arm and stitched his hand to the cuff of the sleeve. Good as new! The kids were excited to find him wearing pajamas the next day. It's good that he is always up high and can't be touched. They will never get a close look at my handiwork. What a hilarious and ridiculous experience. This is a story we will remember and laugh about every Christmas.

I hope things are happy and going well in CA. looking forward to seeing everyone in Arizona.

Love,
Jana

Toothpaste on the Mirror

In 2019 my wife Shauna's father Nate and in July of 2020 her mother Olivia died. I was told that during her parent's sixty-nine years of life together they at times brought up a story of contention that began shortly after their wedding. As the story goes, Nate was accused of miss placing or burning their wedding cards. Olivia was embarrassed because she could not send the wedding thank you notes or mention the gift that was given. These accusations festered from time to time especially when Shauna's brother Tim and she married. The issue lessened in intensity as the years went by.

Several months after Olivia died Shauna and her two children were going over her parent's effects and found the wedding cards neatly tucked away in a safe place with the notes Olivia so carefully placed on the cards sixty-nine years late. They had moved the cards from house to house and city to city during their life together. Shauna and her kids had a wonderful laugh as they reminisced the many times Nate and Olivia quibbled over the whereabouts of these cards.

Bryce R. Petersen wrote, "Small things have a way of growing large when we dwell on them. I learned some very good lessons from Mom and Dad, but the best one I ever learned was about six months after Dad died. Toward the end of my parents' lives, there were times they really didn't get along very well. Dad was not active in the Church, and Mom was impatient with him. They seemed to wear on each other's nerves some of the time. The arguments weren't really serious, but I always felt pressured to take sides, a position I didn't like.

Small offenses have a way of growing large when we dwell on them. One of Mom's common complaints was that Dad splashed toothpaste on the mirror when he brushed his teeth and would never clean it off. It drove her crazy, and she couldn't let it go. I tried to explain that in the grand scheme of life, toothpaste on the mirror wasn't a very big thing. She wasn't mollified. I wished they could get along better, that they could overlook small things and not be so critical of each other and be more forgiving, but that didn't happen very often. Dad died in the spring of 1991. It was a time of grief, especially for Mom. She realized after he was gone that she missed him more than she had anticipated. It was lonesome living alone in that big house; her partner of 62 years was gone. She started talking about him more frequently. As the days turned to weeks and then to months, I visited Mom daily. During one visit her eyes turned watery as she told me of a mistake that she regretted. She reminded me of the toothpaste and how adamant she had been that he was slothful in neglecting to clean up his mess. She had been so angry over such a small thing.

Mom admitted that on the first cleaning day after Dad died, there was toothpaste on the mirror. She cleaned the mirror, but on the second cleaning day, there was more toothpaste on the mirror. The same thing happened on the third and fourth cleaning days as well. Mom realized that she had blamed Dad for the toothpaste on the mirror for many years, but it had been both of them splashing toothpaste. She felt terrible that for years she had been so upset about such a small thing. She freely admitted that her anger had hurt her much worse than it had affected Dad.

I learned from this experience the need for forgiveness and tolerance in our relationships, and I honestly try to be more forgiving on my own. It seems such a waste of time to fret about small offenses. There are more important things to worry about than toothpaste on the mirror."

Bryce R. Petersen, "Toothpaste on the Mirror," Ensign, Sep 2008, 23

In 2021 I received a phone call from George Drysdale, an old Blackfoot High School buddy, I hadn't heard from or seen in about forty years. I was surprised especially since a couple of weeks before his call I found a canceled check written to him for construction.

Our last communication was a chance meeting in the San Jose Airport. He was flying to Hawaii where he built homes for a large development. Besides being a friend from Idaho, he also built an addition on a home I owned when my wife was about to deliver our last child. It was winter, part of the house was open to the elements, access to the home's essentials was limited and her soon-to-be-born son was raising havoc on her not-so-young body. During this time in her life, she was not always a happy momma bear!

George called because he was thinking about the successful basketball team we played together on. It was interesting how he remembered things differently than I did. I didn't know how great a basketball player I was. It sounded so good that I asked him to send me a letter so I could send it to my children. However, I followed Bryce's advice and did not correct George about anything he said concerning my performance in basketball . . .

"I learned from this experience (with my mother) the
need for forgiveness and tolerance in our relationships,
and I honestly try to be more forgiving in my own.
It seems such a waste of time to fret about small offenses."

Bryce R. Petersen

Value of Failure

On a trip to Scotland many years ago I had the opportunity to visit Edinburgh Castle and have lunch in The Elephant House Gourmet Tea & Coffee House and Restaurant overlooking the castle. We were seated in a backroom booth where the author of Harry Potter tended her child and sat writing many of her early novels. Opened in 1995, The house has been made famous as the place of inspiration to writers while overlooking Edinburgh Castle. At the time I didn't appreciate J. K. Rowling's accomplishments (I'm not a fiction reader), hadn't read one of her books and my fondest memories of the visit were finding some of the names of my family members who had served in the queen's military. There were individuals listed with the same spelling as my brother's and my first, middle and last names. I also remember a young waiter from the U.K. that was waiting for our table. We got into a conversation about Scotland and England. He soon became very proud of his homeland and mentioned how his country-owned Scotland. I stood up from the table in fun and started speaking in a loud voice, "This young man would like me to announce that England . . . he stopped me in the middle of the sentence and told me to stop what I was about to say. If I didn't stop he was fearful that he would lose his job and be sent home from his summer job."

Born in Yate, Gloucestershire, England, J. K. (Joanne) Rowling was working as a researcher and bilingual secretary for Amnesty International when she conceived the idea for the Harry Potter series while on a delayed train from Manchester to London in 1990. The seven-year period that followed saw the death of her mother, the birth of her first child, divorce from her first husband, and relative poverty until she finished the first novel in the series, Harry Potter and the Philosopher's Stone, in 1997. Rowling has lived a "rags to riches" life story, in which she progressed from living on state benefits to the 2016 Sunday Times Rich List estimated Rowling's fortune at £600 million, ranking her as the joint 197th richest person in the UK. In October 2010, Rowling was named the "Most Influential Woman in Britain" by leading magazine editors. Wikipedia Joanne once considered herself a failure. A jobless single parent in her late twenties, nearly homeless, she went through the darkest period of her life frightened and almost without hope. Yet when she looks back on this time she emphasizes the benefits of failure.

In 1977 Elder Thomas S. Monson mentioned five Attitudes of Accomplishment: Faith, Work, Courage, Obedience, and Love that can lift us from the darkest periods of our lives (depression, discouragement, and the sense of failure). J.K. Rowling mentions these attitudes (indirectly) during a Commencement Speech she gave at Harvard in 2008.

... "Now, I am not going to stand here and tell you that failure is fun. That period of my life was a dark one, and I had no idea that there was going to be what the press has since represented as a kind of fairy tale resolution. I had no idea then how far the tunnel extended, and for a long time, any light at the end of it was a hope rather than a reality. So why do I talk about the benefits of failure? Simply because failure meant a stripping away of the inessential. I stopped pretending to myself that I was anything other than what I was, and began to direct all my energy (Attitude of Work) into finishing the only work that mattered to me. Had I succeeded at anything else, I might never have found the determination (Attitude of Courage) to succeed in the one arena I believed I truly belonged. I was set free, because my greatest fear had been realized, and I was still alive, and I still had a daughter whom I adored, and I had an old typewriter and a big idea. And so rock bottom became the solid foundation on which I rebuilt my life. You might never fail on the scale I did, but some failure in life is inevitable. It is impossible to live without failing at something unless you live so cautiously that you might as well not have lived at all—in which case, you fail by default. Failure gave me inner security (Attitude of Faith) that I had never attained by passing (school) examinations. Failure taught me things about myself that I could have learned no other way. I discovered that I had a strong will and more discipline (Attitude of Obedience) than I had suspected; I also found out that I had friends whose value (Attitude of Love) was truly above the price of rubies. The knowledge that you have emerged wiser and stronger from setbacks means that you are, ever after, secure in your ability to survive. You will never truly know yourself, or the strength of your relationships until both have been tested by adversity. Such knowledge is a true gift, for all that it is painfully won, and it has been worth more than any qualification (public education) I ever earned." *J.K. Rowling's speech at her Commencement Address at Harvard, June 2008 titled, "The Fringe Benefits of Failure, and the Importance of Imagination.*

Our journey through life will be marked by sorrow and joy, sickness and health—even by failure and accomplishment. Failure, that monstrous scoundrel who would thwart our progress, stifle our initiative, and destroy our dreams, has many faces. Can you recognize them? There is the Face of Fear. Fear erects barriers that separate us from our objectives. We become content with mediocrity when in reality excellence is within our grasp. The comment of the crowd causes us to withdraw from the race, and we retreat to the supposed safety of a sheltered life. A question from the movie Shenandoah points up our cowardice: "If we don't try, we don't do; and if we don't do, then why are we here?" Failure has yet another face, even the Face of Idleness. To daydream, to loaf, to wish without work is to fall into the power of its hypnotic trance.

So subtle, so inviting is the appeal of idleness that one does not know he has yielded his powers to such a deceitful face. "There has never lived a person who was an idler in his own eyes." Consider the Face of Doubt. It too is one of the failure's many masks. Doubt destroys. It chips away at our confidence, undermines our testimony, and erodes our resistance to evil. Shun its winsome smile.

No enumeration of failure's many faces would be complete without the Face of Sin. This culprit plays for keeps. The stakes are high. Paul declared: "The wages of sin is death." (Rom. 6:23.) And who can disregard the word of the Lord. *Faces and Attitudes, Elder Thomas S. Monson, Council of the Twelve, Sept 1977, Era.*

I now have a change of heart as I look back so many years ago not appreciating the opportunity of sitting in the booth where J.K. Rowling sat those many hours overlooking Edinburgh Castle "A jobless single parent in her late twenties, nearly homeless, and going through the darkest period of her life frightened and almost without hope." I am now in awe and humbled how she overcame her feelings of failure and the real-life story of success she can share with the world along with the wonderful stories of the fictional Harry Potter.

In the game of life, a second effort is often required. The happy life is not ushered in at any age to the sound of drums and trumpets. It grows upon us year by year, little by little until at last, we realize that we have it. It is achieved in individuals not by flights to the moon or Mars, but by a body of work done so well that we can lift our heads with assurance and look the world in the eye. Of this be sure: You do not find the happy life . . . you make it. *Thomas S. Monson, 1977*

Bears

During its first century, Yellowstone National Park was known as the place to see and interact with bears. Hundreds of people gathered nightly to watch black bears feed on garbage in the park's dumps. Enthusiastic visitors fed bears along the roads and behaved recklessly to take photographs. Beginning in 1931, park managers began recording bear-inflicted human injuries and incidents of property damage each year in Yellowstone. In 1960, the park implemented a bear management program directed primarily at black bears designed to reduce injuries, property damages and to re-establish bears in a natural state. The plan included expanding visitor education about bear behavior and the proper way to store food and other bear attractants; installing bear-proof garbage cans; strictly prohibiting the feeding of bears, and removing potentially dangerous bears, habituated bears, and bears that damaged property in search of food. The open-pit garbage dumps remained open. In 1970, Yellowstone initiated a more intensive program that included eliminating open-pit garbage dumps inside the park with the intention of returning bears to a natural diet of plant and animal food. In 1983, the park implemented a new grizzly bear management program that emphasized habitat protection in backcountry areas. Yellowstone Park established "bear management areas" that restricted recreational use where grizzly bears were known to concentrate, to prevent human-caused displacement of bears from prime food sources, and to decrease the risk of bear-caused human injury in areas with high levels of bear activity. This program continues today. 2018-2019 Yellowstone National Park Annual Report During the 1950s and '60s, I lived within two hours of Yellowstone National Park and my family would do a day drive through the park. When traveling with my father, he would insist that there would be no food in the car, no windows open if the bears stopped us and we did not camp within the boundaries of the park. The only bear I have seen in the wild backcountry was during a mule deer hunting trip when we walked to the top of a mountain and looking into a ravine next to another mountain saw a black bear running as fast as it could through the ravine and up a mountain away from us. It took binoculars to get a good view of the bear. People often encourage bears to come out of the forest by providing food without realizing it. When bears become used to these food sources and have frequent contact with humans they are often considered "nuisance bears." This is bad news for the bears. Relocating a nuisance bear is nearly impossible and frequently they must be killed. The most common sources of food that attract bears are pet food, bird feeders, barbecue grills, garbage, household trash containers, open dumpsters, and campsites with accessible food and food wastes. My brother-in-law, Tim Karren, was hunting deer in Idaho and a "nuisance bear" met him on a trail with no fear in his eyes. I met Tim for the first time several years later and I asked him where he got the black bear hide proudly displayed on his family room wall.

Yellowstone was the first officially recognized national park and at first, the public didn't want to see that much land designated strictly for the use of recreation and pleasure. Especially because it was being paid for by tax dollars. So, to attract more park visitors bear feedings started to become extremely popular. The exact date these feedings started is unknown but records dating back to as early as 1909 when F. Dumont Smith visited the Yellowstone Lake Hotel. He wrote about how upset he was that he and his girlfriend didn't get to ride in the "garbage cart" that would take old food scraps out to feed the bears. There were multiple feeding platforms strategically placed all over Yellowstone, as well as a few other parks like Yosemite and Sequoia. They would even place them near hotels and advertised being able to see bears feeding and eat a meal in the hotel within an hour. The most common name you will see when researching this topic is Horace Albright. He was the superintendent of Yellowstone starting in 1919 and he was a huge fan of the bear feedings. When he took the position he made the human-animal interaction one of his top priorities. He felt he had "a duty to present wildlife as a spectacle" for the many tourists that attend the parks. He even went as far as to open two zoos within the park so that people could get an up-close look at the many animals seen in the park. Albright is said to be the one that built the bear feeding platform with wooden benches set up all around it and only a small safety ditch between onlookers and the hungry bears outside Old Faithful where he had a big sign above it saying "Lunch Counter for Bears." Just after dinnertime park ranger, Philip Martindale, would mount his horse and back it up to where he was only 30 feet away from the bears and proceeded to teach about the bear's biology among other things. When cars started to be allowed into the park the bears looked at them like big trash cans filled with dinner. These bears would earn the fitting nickname "Hold-up Bears" because they would essentially hold up passing cars until they either fed them or worse. It has taken decades for the bears to stop "holding up" cars for any food they might have on hand, surprisingly it took just as long for visitors of the park to stop hanging sweets and other tasty treats out their window. I remember tales that bears used to deliberately halt car traffic in the park—all the better to send the cubs scampering among Chevy station wagons and Ford sedans, begging for food. Critter jams and especially bear jams were a big part of my first trip to Yellowstone. Bears fed on marshmallows and Fig Newtons, slipped through narrow openings in car windows, as kids squealed and Mom worried aloud. All innocent fun, until in one bear jam, I learned the meaning of the saying, "God looks after fools and children." There were a man and woman in a Volkswagen Bug, right in front of us. Traffic wasn't moving, and the bear activity seemed to be many cars ahead, so the couple grabbed a camera, got out of the car, and trotted down the road for an Eastman Kodak moment. Both doors were left open in the car. Soon enough, a big brown bear emerged from the woods to investigate and crawl into the back seat, where he busily started excavating and rooting around for food. That little Volkswagen started rocking and rolling, and that's when the male driver came back. He was mad. He was furious. He was nuts. "Kids," said Dad, "don't watch this, because it could get ugly." Well, of course, we watched. The driver of the Volkswagen started kicking the bear, hard, right in the keister. The bear, which could have destroyed the driver with a single paw swipe, had limited room to maneuver in the back seat of the Bug, so he left through the opposite door and kept ongoing. I realized that I'd just witnessed a minor miracle—a fool who wasn't eaten alive, as he well deserved. It could be rationally argued that visitors shouldn't be allowed to get out of the car until they've read *Death in Yellowstone, Lee Whittlesey's* compilation of 300 deaths, or how people needlessly died by being boiled, scalded, drowned, gored, frozen, struck by lightning, knocked off a cliff, eaten by a grizzly, shot, murdered or run over by another tourist. *Feeding the Bears*

—*A Trip Down Memory Lane, 2017.*

The preferred foods for black bears are nuts, acorns, fruit, insects, and succulent greens. Meat and less succulent greens are eaten when preferred foods are scarce. Black bears like large forests, are 4 to 7 feet long and weigh 125 to 500 pounds. They have small eyes, rounded ears, a long snout, a short tail, and have shaggy black or brown or blond hair. The American black bear is found only in North America, sees in color, and has good vision closeup. Hearing exceeds human frequency ranges and probably twice the sensitivity. Their smelling ability is extremely good. They are commonly thought to have the keenest sense of smell in the animal kingdom and estimates of the range of their sense of smell vary widely from over a mile to between 18 and 20 miles. One of the more intelligent mammals, their navigation ability is superior to humans and they have an excellent long-term memory. They are usually silent, do not threaten by growling (except in movies in which sounds are dubbed in), and display a variety of grunts in amiable situations or loud blowing noises when frightened. They can swim at least a mile and run over 30 mph level, up or downhill. Black bears are comfortable around humans and mostly prefer not to be seen or heard. Predatory attacks on humans by black bears are extremely rare and a "disproportionate number" of attacks by bears on humans are related to interactions with dogs.

Lynn Rogers, research scientist for the Wildlife Research Institute and founder of the North American Bear Center

According to my oldest son Chris' memory, the year was 1985 when he was ten and his brother was nine years old we paired up with their uncle Mark Gardner and his two about the same age boys and camped near Yosemite. As I recall we parked our vehicle in a designated lot and took a bus that dropped us off at a hiking trail. Mostly I remember dry hot days and cool to cold nights, dust, glaring sun, granite rock everywhere that reflected the sun's heat, and beautiful clear lakes scattered along the way. We had seen bear tracks during our hike and were very careful not to have food items left in our tents. Since there were no "bear safe" storage facilities available at night we strung all our food items with a rope as high as we could between two trees. The tree trunks were small enough in diameter that we felt a bear could not get enough of a claw hold to climb the trees. I believe it was our second night of camping in the early morning that I was awakened by grunting sounds and then heard rustling around the camp. I jumped out of my sleeping bag, zipped open the tent, and making loud noises appeared in the bright moon-lit night barefooted in my tidy whiteys stumbling around our campsite. I was having one of those stupid go-get them moments that proves again "God often looks after fools and children." We had no dogs with us which may have been a saving grace and fortunately, black bears are usually not confrontational. I was angry enough that if I could have found one of those bears I would have also tried to kick it in its keister. Examining the area later in the morning we figured out that the adult bears had their darling little cubs climb the trees and pull on the ropes until our food became their dinner as it came falling like manna from heaven. The only food item left we could find were packages of hot chocolate with tooth marks in each one. Evidently bears will eat almost anything except they don't like the taste of sugar-free items. Uncle Mark hiked towards the road to retrieve the car and the rest of us lugged the camping gear back to the road with no food but plenty of cool water with or without diet hot chocolate mix.

My uncle Bud Rich, a rancher, used to tell the story about shooting a bear during a hunting trip. Looking at the bear after they had hung it in a tree and removed its hide they left the carcass behind. Reason: the skinned bear looked so much like a human body they didn't have the stomach to eat it.

"Among mortals, second thoughts are wisest" Euripides 480-406 B.C.

Tragedy and The Miracle
Of Forgiveness

In the spring of 1968, I was preparing to graduate from the University of Idaho and had received an NIH grant to start graduate school at Purdue University in the Department of Animal Science. About that time, I was also informed by the Selective Service System that I had been classified as a 1-A and eligible for military service. Not knowing exactly what that meant I visited my draft board in Blackfoot Idaho during spring break. My question to her was whether going to graduate school was a poor choice if I were going to be drafted. She told me a lot that I don't remember; but, the most important things I do remember given so much in these words. "You are going into a field of graduate work that a deferment at this time is appropriate and do you see a lot of your friends 'dragging main street' at night in town? If you're doing what you say you will be doing and your friends continue doing what they're doing—they're going first."

Uncle Sam has called upon its fighting-age citizens as far back as anyone alive could recall, as both World

WALTER R. HOGE, DVM

Wars and the Korean War utilized draftees. The Selective
Service Act of 1917 reframed the process, outlawing clauses
like purchasing and expanding upon deferments. Military
service was something that, voluntary or not, living
generations had in common.1 It was the Selective Service
Act of 1917 that directly led to one of the West's most
amazing tales of a bloody shootout, four dead, a manhunt
spanning hundreds of miles, and one of the longest prison
sentences in Arizona history. 2018 marked the hundredth
anniversary of an event that there are still unanswered
questions and the real truth is a GOK (God only knows).

Before dawn on a bitterly cold morning on Feb. 10,
1918, a posse consisting of a county sheriff, two deputies,
and a U.S. marshal was there to arrest the four men in the
cabin below. In the dark, they surrounded it where Jeff
Power, his sons Tom and John, and a hired hand named
Tom Sisson lived there working a mining claim. The
brothers were wanted for draft dodging. Jeff Power and
Sisson were wanted for perjury. The Power family had a
young colt, which was belled so they could find it in the
mornings. They heard the bell on the colt and thought a
mountain lion was stalking it. Jeff Power walked outside
carrying his rifle. Someone yelled from the dark, Throw up
your hands! He put his rifle between his knees and put up
his hands. A bullet slammed into his chest. Who shot first
no one will ever know. There was a lull of about a minute
after the first shot and then in three minutes about 25
shots were fired and the gun battle was over. The Powers
and Sisson had no idea why they had come after them. Jeff
Power and three of the four officers were killed. Realizing

among the dead were officers and it was not safe to stay there, the Powers boys and Tom Sisson decided to flee to Mexico.

The event that happened around the end of 1917 that set the stage for the shootout was that the Supreme Court heard arguments about the Selective Service Act—the draft law—and voted to uphold it the first week of January 1918. The draft law that Tom and John Power were breaking, was a misdemeanor, not a felony. It wasn't a big crime. The maximum sentence for failing to register for the draft was a year in prison. And the Power brothers were solidly on the federal government's least-wanted list. More than 3 million men had failed to register.

After the shooting ended, the brothers and Sisson leaned over Jeff Power and knew the wound was fatal. They examined the bodies in front of the cabin and discovered who they had killed. They had no idea why they had come after them. What they did know was that they were officers and it was not safe to stay there. They decided to run for Mexico, reasoning the law was trying to kill them. Thousands of men hunted the fugitives, on horseback, in trucks and cars, with two military planes and the cavalry patrols even tore down the Mexican border fence. The brothers and Sisson made it into Mexico but in the end, they were not captured. They surrendered. Filthy, starving, and shoeless, with no water. John's damaged eye socket crawled with maggots. They just couldn't go any further.

The three of them were tried together; the trial lasted only five days. The whole thing reminded many of a circus with the only evidence not being presented was that the first shot may have come from the deputies. The three men were sentenced to life in prison. Arizona had abolished the death penalty the year before. On April 20, 1960, forty-two years after the shootings, the Power brothers received a full parole hearing and received clemency, and were released from prison 2.

Glenn Kempton was one of the nineteen orphaned children from Arizona's 1918 deadliest gunfights. He was also one who was able to forgive the Power brothers for having to grow up deprived of a father and being subject to the usual prejudices, hates, and bitterness that would naturally surround a young boy under such circumstances. He has been gracious enough to tell me the story in his way.

As a young boy in my early teens, there grew in my heart bitterness and hatred toward the confessed slayer of my Father, for Tom Power had admitted killing my Dad. The years swept by, I grew up, but still, that heavy feeling stayed inside me. High school ended and then I received a call to go to the Eastern States Mission. There my knowledge and testimony of the gospel grew rapidly, as all of my time was spent studying and preaching it. One day while reading the New Testament, I came to Matthew, fifth chapter, verses 43 to 45. Here it was, the words of the Savior saying we should forgive. This applied to me. I read those verses again and again and it still meant forgiveness. Not very long after this, I found in the 64th section of the Doctrine and Covenants, verses 9 and 10 more of the Savior's words. And then there were these timely words of

President John Taylor: "Forgiveness is in advance of Justice where repentance is concerned."

I didn't know whether or not Tom Powers had repented but I did know now that I had an appointment to make after I returned home, and I resolved before I left the mission field to do just that. After returning home, I met and married a fine Latter-day saint girl, and the Lord blessed our home with five lovely children. The years were passing rapidly and the Lord had been good to us, yet guilt arose within me every time I thought of the appointment I had not kept. In 1954 just shortly before Christmas, a season when the love of Christ abounds and the spirit of giving and forgiving gets inside of us, my wife and I were in Phoenix on a short trip. Having concluded our business in the middle of the second afternoon, we started home. As we rode along, I expressed the desire to detour and return home via Florence, for that is where the state prison is located. My wife readily assented. It was after visiting hours when we arrived but I went on inside and asked for the warden. I was directed to his office.

After I had introduced myself and expressed a desire to meet and talk to Tom Powers a puzzled expression came over the warden's face, but after only a slight hesitation, he said, "I'm sure that can be arranged." Whereupon he dispatched a guard down into the compound who soon returned with Tom. We were introduced and led into the parole room where we had a long talk. We went back to the cold, gray February morning thirty years before, re-enacting that whole terrible tragedy. We talked for perhaps an hour and a half. Finally, I said, "Tom, you made a mistake for which you owe a debt to society for which I feel you must continue to pay, just the same as I must continue to pay the price for having been reared without a father." Then I stood and extended my hand. He stood and took it. I continued, "With all my heart, I forgive you for the awful thing that has come into our lives." He bowed his head and I left him there. I don't know how he felt then, and I don't know how he feels now, but my witness to you is that it is a glorious thing when bitterness and hatred go out of your heart and forgiveness comes in. I thanked the warden for his kindness, and as I walked out the door and down that long flight of steps I knew that forgiveness was better than revenge, for I had experienced it.

As we drove toward home in the gathering twilight, a sweet and peaceful calm came over me. Out of pure gratitude, I placed my arm around my wife, who understood, for I know that we had now found a broader, richer, and more abundant life.

All conscience acts set in motion changes in a person's life. Like the Power family, some create life changes that will affect every day of one's life. Others might nag you from time to time, make you feel some guilt, wish that you had never made such a decision, and wish you could turn back the clock. On June 27th, 2019 I wrote this letter concerning a thought I requested be presented to my 55th year High School Class Reunion. I was my senior class vice president in high school. Our president Jerry Smith died the year before, I had a stroke on April 23, 2019, and felt it wise not to travel to Blackfoot Idaho.

Dear Tom Richardson,

There is only one thought you might share with our class that has bothered me every time we prepare for a class reunion. When I ran for senior class vice president I did it because I felt I could do a better job than the other candidate, Jim Smith. This was not a particularly bright move on my part since I'm not good at speaking in front of an audience or of a political nature. This decision might have been influenced by my attending the American Legions Gem Boy's State in Boise (think I have the name correct). Here we learned about running for political office and contributing to our community. Not long after graduation, we lost Jim in Vietnam. My parents were good friends with Jim's and it seemed like every time I was home with my parents during social events the Smiths were there. Jim's mom would always say to me, "Rich, would you turn around for me? I would like to imagine what Jim would have looked like if he were here." This request would tear my heart out. And every thought of a reunion brings me back to thoughts of Jim. Why did I run against him, he couldn't have made a worse VP than me, he would more than likely have lived near Blackfoot where he could help our class more, and it would have been nice for his parents to have added Vice President of the Blackfoot High School Senior Class to their memories of Jim.

I hope there is a good turnout this year. we were fortunate to have grown up in an isolated and protected area and the teachers helped us be able to take on the world no matter where we landed. Please plan another class reunion. I noticed this year's event has a wheelchair ramp—that boosts my confidence that I will make the next one. If you get the opportunity, give a toast to Jim Smith for me. *"With all my heart, I forgive you . . ." Glenn Kempton—simple words that can change the world*

1-How War Works, Samantha Peterson 04-29-2020,

2-Arizona's Deadliest Gunfight, Heidi Osselaer,

3-Glenn Kempton, The Miracle of Forgiveness, Spencer W. Kimball, 290-293 1969

Who Packed My Parachute

Charles Plumb was a jet pilot in the US Navy. On his seventy-sixth combat mission, he was shot down in Vietnam and parachuted into enemy territory. He was captured and survived six years in captivity. He tells a story about a time he was sitting in a restaurant in Kansas City. A man about two tables away kept looking over at him but Plumb didn't recognize him. A few minutes later the man stood up and walked over, looked down at Charles, pointed his finger in his face, and said "You're Captain Plumb." He looked up and said, "Yes sir, I'm Captain Plumb." The man said, "You flew jet fighters in Vietnam. You were on the aircraft carrier, Kitty Hawk. You were shot down. You parachuted into enemy hands and spent six years as a prisoner of war." "How in the world did you know all that?" asked Plumb. The man replied, "Because, I packed your parachute." Plumb was amazed—and gratefully said, "If the chute you packed hadn't worked I wouldn't be here today . . ."

Where would you be today if it weren't for those around you that nurtured and cared for you with the, ". . . aim for an education that would help develop resources in you that would contribute to your well-being as long as life endures; to develop the power of self-mastery that you may never be a slave to indulgence or other weaknesses, to develop (strong) manhood, beautiful womanhood that in every child and every youth may be found at least the promise of a friend, a companion, one who later may be fit for husband or wife, an exemplary father or a loving intelligent mother, one who can face life with courage, meet disaster with fortitude, and face death without fear." *David O. McKay.*

Who has helped pack your parachute? I hadn't started school yet when my family moved to the Wilcox Apartments across the street from Bingham Memorial Hospital in Blackfoot Idaho. This arrangement made it easy for Dad to do his hospital rounds and eventually he purchased an office building in the same location. Near the apartments there was a ditch with high banks that I recall was not often full of water. My friend and I made this our place of building forts, conducting war, and other imaginary feats of grandeur. One day we were playing war by throwing dirt clods at one another and noticed an elderly woman just over the top of the ditch working in her garden. We joined forces and started throwing the dirt clods at her (boy I must have been very young). I remember her being out of range from our trajectory and not hitting her. However, it was not long before my father had a good visit with me discussing how we should always respect others (even if they looked like a scarecrow put there to scare away the birds—which was my excuse) and I found myself fearfully walking up her sidewalk with a handful of flowers to beg her forgiveness.

The Fort Hall Indian Reservation is situated between Blackfoot and Pocatello Idaho. During my childhood, some of the youth on the reservation attended Blackfoot and some attended Pocatello schools. It seemed to me like most of these students would attend school until they were sixteen (all Idaho students were legally required to attend till this age) and then drop out. I vagally remember getting to know several of these students being in my classes and especially in Vocational Agriculture where we worked together in the shop and did field trips together. My parents, especially my mom, showed a lot of interest in my Ag classes. I raised pigs and had a beef cow for projects. My uncle Bud would take my cow to range on the Indian Reservation each spring and winter her on his ranch. I learned great respect for our Native Americans and was never led to believe that my heritage was better or more special than others. The stories and experiences my parents shared with me about the Indians enriched my thoughts about my heritage.

My mother's family lived in Pingree Idaho and owned land that was within the bounds of the Indian Reservation. There were springs on the property, a fish hatchery and the water flowed directly into the Snake River. It was a wonderful place to explore and try my luck at fishing. Mom would tell me stories of the experiences her family had with the Indians. One of her favorite pictures was when she was dressed in a ceremonial Indian costume. Mom was always respectful and discussed her family's wonderful experiences growing up in the area and some of the struggles the Indians had. At times they would ask her family for help and my grandfather would share with them the food they were raising on their ranch.

My father was an MD and he told me that he would rather care for an Indian than the rest of us. In my dad's eyes when an Indian visited his clinic he was truly in need of care, communicated his needs without a lot of talk, was polite and respectful to dad, listened, and showed appreciation for his care. One day I was in dad's office and he came in and sat down with me after he had seen a patient. He was noticeably embarrassed. He told me that he had just seen an Indian patient with a broken hand that he had cast several weeks before. The man had not been making his recheck appointments and dad spoke with him about how important it was that the cast be rechecked and the many reasons why it was important. The man was respectful, did not make up excuses why he hadn't come in for rechecks, and "didn't say much."

After the examination dad accompanied him to the reception area and the local sheriff was waiting to take him back to jail.

I had the opportunity to attend Purdue University in West Lafayette, Indiana. During my sophomore year, an African American woman joined my class and her husband became a member of the faculty. I became friendly with her and during idle conversion, I used the "N" word. She jumped all over me for using this word and had little to do with me for the rest of my days in veterinary school. It took a long time for me to find out what her problem was. Here I was from Idaho with no clue about race, segregation, or protesting these issues. I felt I was being respectful calling her race the "N" word since on every application I had filled out relating to education was the section that asked if I were Caucasian, Oriental, Negroid, or other. As time went on I became more aware of these issues as I saw student protests on campus. Purdue University had both a student and West Lafayette LDS religious services available. During the height of segregation protests of the sixties, the student ward was informed that there may be protesters entering our building during Sunday services. The question was how we should respond if it did occur. We were counseled to greet the protestors at the door of the chapel and invite them in one by one and sit down with them and proceed with our meeting. We should take the opportunity to get to know them and discuss our faith with them and explain what was occurring during the meeting. It never happened, but I remember being scared and confused about why people just couldn't get along and look after each other as my parents had taught me. In Acts 10:34-35, Peter said, "Of a truth, I perceive that God is no respecter of persons: but in every nation, he that feareth him, and worketh righteousness, is accepted with him." This means that God shows no partiality.

Some of the other special lessons I was taught by my mom and dad were:

- It is important to have an understanding that we all have a great legacy that came before us from God our Father in Heaven and from our experiences as His spirit children, and that we exercised our agency to come to this earth, and this legacy continues down to the homes in which we grew up and the life we are currently living.

- If you do something—do it to the best of your ability. When I did poorly on an assignment my mother seemed to always be there to see that I understood why and helped me correct the mistakes.

- Use care with what comes out of your mouth. One day I was down in the basement attempting a task and my language got out of hand. Mom said nothing at the time but a few days later mentioned that she had no idea her son would ever have a desire to have such words come out of his mouth. That comment burned to the core and it has stuck with me to this day.

- Dad taught me that when you have been given a special title in your community (policeman, fireman, doctor, judge . . .) you have the responsibility to set an example as a good citizen, not dishonor your position or take advantage of those in which you serve.

- You aren't the center of the universe. God loves and cares for all his children the same. Be careful not to become prideful and too good for your britches.

- Always be nice to others—it's better to have a friend than an enemy.

- When you work for someone always give a 110% effort.

- Show interest in the task at hand—you might just learn something new.

- Don't cut off your nose to spite your face— needlessly being over-reactive and making it worse.

- If you have a frowny face never let it stay—quickly turn it upside down and smile that frown away. -If you have trouble with a teacher at school—what did you do to offend her/him?

- If you are offended let it go. If you let it fester it can destroy your life, but not the offenders.

- You can lose your fortune, liberty, or health— nobody can take away your education or wisdom.

Captain Charles Plumb thought a lot about the unseen Navy shipman and realized that these anonymous sailors who packed the parachutes held the pilots' lives in their hands. Yet the pilots never gave these sailors a second thought; never even said hello, let alone said thanks. "I wondered how many times I might have passed him on board the Kitty Hawk. I wondered how many times I might have seen him and not even said "good morning", "how are you", or anything because, you see, I was a fighter pilot and he was just a sailor. How many hours did he spend on that long wooden table in the bowels of that ship weaving the shrouds and folding the silks of those chutes?" *Who Packs*

Your Parachute? September 21, 2016, Iain Smith Leadership and Management Trainer.

My mother and father spent hours caring for my needs during the time that my life and happiness was literally in their hands and I am embarrassed at the many times I have seen them and not even said good morning, how are you, or anything except expressing to them my perceived selfish needs at the time, because, you see, I thought I was (smarter than them) and they were just keeping the ship afloat and oftentimes seemed to me only in my way.

> *If the knowledge and wisdom my parents helped pack into my chute before I left home hadn't worked in society—when the chute needed to be opened during my life there would not have been such soft landings.*

Helping Hands Can
Save The Day

Thousands of years ago, the Greek storyteller Aesop told of a father who noticed similar problems among his many sons. They always seemed to be quarreling, despite their father's pleadings for unity. One day he gathered his sons around him, showed them a bundle of sticks bound with cords, and asked them to break it. The oldest son strained and strained with all his might but was unable to break the bundle, no matter how hard he tried. Then the father removed one stick from the bundle and asked his littlest son to break it—which he did easily. The lesson was clear to all of them: alone we are weak and easily broken, but together we are strong. What's true with sticks is also true that a group of humans can accomplish a lot if they just work together. A husband-wife duo from Florida led by example on July 12, 2017, when they urged nearly 80 strangers to form a human chain into the ocean to save a group of swimmers caught in a rip current at Panama City Beach.

Derek and Jessica Simmons demonstrated the presence of mind when they spotted nine swimmers struggling to stay afloat off the coast. The couple was at the beach for dinner. Jessica immediately grabbed hold of a discarded boogie board and began swimming towards the trapped swimmers while her husband stayed behind to gather beachgoers to form a human chain. More and more people joined hands and created a long (daisy) chain. A couple of young boys and a few adults swam in the ocean to help out the youngsters. The incident happened around 6.30 p.m. EDT, and the lifeguards had left for the day. The people who initially tried saving the boys were also caught up in the unruly waves. "We grabbed the kids and tried to start swimming in and it just kept pulling us back," Brittany Monroe, one of the swimmers who tried to help the drowning boys told *ABC News*. "The water was really strong (on Saturday) but where we were it wasn't pulling us. When we got to where the kids were, that's when we realized we were stuck."

The human chain grew from five people to 80 people and saved the day. Derek said the gesture of the people coming together to form the chain proved humans could come together at a time of distress despite the differences and intolerances. "A lot of people were like, 'There's no way we're getting in the water, we're going to get swept out,' but I guess they just swallowed the pride pill and they just got in," Derek said. "It was pretty amazing stuff for it to be different races, different genders, different ages; everybody got together to help."

Even as advances in communication help people around the world connect like never before, it also seems that division and discord around the world are reaching new levels. Differing beliefs, values, and convictions too often lead to hostility and even conflict. We may wonder how we can find peace and security in what can be an unsettling world. Also, what's true with sticks in a bundle and people joining hands to form a daisy chain to save stranded swimmers in a rip current is also true of marriages, families, communities, and nations. No matter how strong we may be individually, our strength and security are greatly multiplied when we stand shoulder to shoulder, hand in hand with each other. This doesn't mean that we must let go of our deeply held convictions. Nor does it necessarily mean that we ignore our differences. We need those differences. Unity is not sameness; it's making wise use of the uniqueness everyone can contribute. Unity means being quick to forgive and ready to set aside our self-interest. It means extending compassion and understanding. It's not easy, but if we have each other's best interests at heart if we are patient and respectful, then bound together by cords of love, we can withstand—and achieve—almost anything. That's the power of unity. *Music & the Spoken Word, 2017-06-04 #4,577.*

During the rescue of the trapped people in the rip current Derek said; "I thought of using the particular technique because it has already been proven effective in the animal kingdom and is frequently used by ants. The only thing that popped into my mind was if you've ever watched ants when one of their babies is in trouble and can't move, they start making a chain to pass them down the line to get them to safety. That's the only thing I was thinking of, if we're arm to arm, we can get them." It is true individual ants can't accomplish much, but ants working together in a colony are capable of extraordinary feats. Cooperative ants form bridges with their bodies, carry large objects, form life rafts during a flood and in *August 2014 Helen McCreery* published an article describing Southeast Asian ants that form cooperative organized lines (daisy chain) by linking their mandibles to the preceding ant's abdomen to transport large insects to their nests. Common behavior among ants? Hardly. After speaking with *California State University entomologist Terry McGlynn,* that "It's a particular kind of behavior that ant experts haven't seen before."

There is a proverb:

'United we stand divided we fall.'
Ten's sticks together unbreakable.
Can be broken easily if given to all.
Wind easily blows the dust. But cannot move the rock.
Birds trapped in a net, united.
Along with the net, flew the flock.
As well, if people are united. For valid and right cause.
There can't be any reason.
Their efforts will pause. S. D. Tiwari
One pair of hands often fails to save from the surf.
Many hands held tight in a chain saves many from the tide.
One ant accomplishes little to care for the nest.
Many a mandible latched to another's belly.
Forms a long chain that brings food to the rest.

WR Hoge, 08/17/2018

"*The lesson was clear to all of them: alone we are weak and easily broken, but together we are strong.*"
United we stand, divided we fall . . . Aesop

Greyhounds and Al Capone

Greyhound racing in the United States is coming to a close. Since the peak of dog racing in 1985, state laws have led to the closure of racetracks across the country. After Florida's tracks closed at the end of 2020, and Iowa and Arkansas' close by the end of 2022, only two active commercial racetracks will remain—both in West Virginia. These closures are occurring from reduced attendance, the increased availability of more casinos, stigma from past doping dogs and fixed races, and public outcry of animal abuse. When I started working for Dr. Hylton at Camden Pet Hospital in 1976 he introduced me to my first greyhound. He raised them and they would come to the hospital for treatment. I needed to become more familiar with the breed and how they differed from other dogs. Even though they are superb athletes with great endurance and the fastest dog on this planet they are also fragile. For example, they have very little body fat and a thin hair coat which makes them susceptible to hypothermia. Therefore, when they are placed under an anesthetic and during the recovery phase it is important to keep a warm blanket on them. They are also prone to stress fractures of their feet and legs from the forces placed on them while running on a circular track. There is concern about what will happen to greyhounds that are retired from a race track. Most are retired by 3-4 years of age and their normal life expectancy is 12-15. There have been accusations of selling retired dogs for research and the illegal killing of thousands of them. A prosecutor in one case called these events a "Dachau for dogs." I became aware of these activities when attending veterinary conferences and visiting with the greyhound adoption organizations that were trying to find homes for these retired dogs.

The greyhound breed goes back in history over 4000 years. The ancestors of the modern greyhounds were used for hunting in ancient Egypt, the Arab world, Persia, and the Greco-Roman epoch. In the 5th century, a Greek soldier Xenophon who was Socrates' pupil wrote a manual on hunting with dogs. Fast hunting dogs were a prized possession of pharaohs, kings, and ancient aristocracy. The hunting breed was even mentioned in the Bible—Proverbs 30-31 "A lion which is strongest among beasts, and turneth not away for any; a greyhound; he goat also; and a king, against whom there is no rising up."

The greyhound is a beautiful animal well-bred for the functions it is to perform. It is the fastest dog breed averaging 39 miles per hour and they are blessed with a keen sense of sight that aids them in chasing fast-moving prey. It is propelled by very long foot bones (for leverage) and high muscle mass. Their rump and thigh muscles are larger than those of most other breeds. A deep chest maximizes lung power and holds an especially large heart.

The direct ancestor of greyhound racing was a sport of coursing, which was very popular in medieval Europe for centuries. The coursing was a chase of live prey across open country. The prey usually was small animals like hares and foxes. The greyhounds were followed by the judges and spectators on horses. The first formal rules of greyhound coursing were established by Queen Elizabeth I in the 16th century. That's why the greyhound racing is called the "Sport of Queens." The sport of queens was a favorite pastime of the European aristocracy. It was not available for the common folks who could not afford to keep the horses and greyhounds. The modern history of greyhound racing started in 19th century England when somebody came up with an idea of a circular racing course. That idea was met with great enthusiasm from the public. They could conveniently sit on the stands and watch the dogs running around circular racing tracks chasing a mechanical rabbit.

In 1912 an inventor by the name of Owen P. Smith perfected the mechanical lure by making it electrically powered. It became easy to control the speed of the lure keeping the rabbit always at a close distance in front of the dogs. Smith's invention was first tried with great success in 1919 on the greyhound racing track in Emeryville California. This invention started a chain of events that resulted in the well-known mobster Al Capone being sentenced to 11 years at Alcatraz Penitentiary in 1933, the death in 1939 of one of Capone's attorneys, Easy Eddie, and Eddies son having an airport named after him in 1963.

Easy Eddie was one of Al Capone's lawyers. However, Eddie was already a successful lawyer when he began working for Capone. In St. Louis, Eddie represented Owen P. Smith an inventor who made the first mechanical rabbit to be used at dog races. Eddie helped Smith get his designs patented and then later used his legal skills to gain full rights to the invention. Eddie got a percentage of the gate money in exchange for the use of the mechanical rabbit. At the time, gambling on dogs was big business and Eddie was one of the beneficiaries. He and his wife Selma, along with their three children bought a nice home in St. Louis that had a swimming pool and a family car. But the marriage didn't last and Eddie divorced his wife and took his son Edward to Chicago. He left behind Selma and his two young daughters Patricia and Marilyn.

In Chicago, Eddie's success in the dog and horse racing business continued. Successful businesses like this would need protection and at this time in Chicago Al Capone's gang essentially owned the city. Eddy became one of Capone's trusted lawyers and helped legally defend the famous gangster. Capone's empire was said to be built on racketeering, bootlegged alcohol, race track fixed races, gambling rings, and prostitution. Eddie was paid extremely well for his legal services but deep inside he worried about his son Edward.

Eddie's lifestyle was starting to catch up with him. His marriage had gone sour, he had taken advantage of the inventor of the mechanical rabbit, the money he received was not clean and he was involved professionally with Al Capone which helped him continue his illegal activities. He was falling into the trap described in Psalms 141:10 "Let the wicked fall into their nets . . ." Eddie must have felt guilt, was remorseful and wanted to attempt restitution for the way he was living his life. One of his first attempts to right his wrongs was to meet with Frank J. Wilson of the treasury department and agreed to help the government convict Capone of tax evasion. He was believed to have given the government key financial records of Capone's operation and also how to decipher them. Finally, Eddie was able to tell the government that Capone had bribed the jury in his trial which resulted in the judge changing the jury at the last moment. In *The People v. Al Capone,* Capone was convicted and sentenced to 11 years at Alcatraz Penitentiary in 1933.

He also encouraged his son Edward to leave the area and join the military. In 1937, Easy Eddie's son was accepted to the Annapolis Naval Academy in Maryland. Here Edward picked up the nickname "Butch".

Easy Eddie knew that the mob doesn't forget a wrong and they would come after him. He carried in his suit pocket these items: a Spanish-made .32-caliber semiautomatic pistol, the rosary, the crucifix, a religious medallion, and a prophetic poem which leads one to believe he knew his past would eventually catch up with him. On November 8, 1939, the once pristine hood of a Lincoln-Zephyr was crushed upon impact at the corner of Ogden Avenue and Rockwell Street in Chicago. Neighbors were slowly pulled out of their houses by the magnetic force of their curiosity. They circled the wreckage as the police arrived. What they found was a car riddled with bullets. Inside the car, police found a well-dressed man, Easy Eddie, slumped almost horizontal in the front seat. In his coat pocket was a Spanish-made .32-caliber semiautomatic pistol that was loaded but had not been fired. Upon further investigation, they also found a rosary, a crucifix, a religious medallion, and a magazine clipping of that prophetic poem which read: "The clock of life is wound but once, and no man has the power, to tell just when the hands will stop at late or early hour. Now is the only time you own. Live, love, toil with a will. Place no faith in time. For the clock may soon be still."

As for Eddie's son butch on February 20, 1942, he became a pilot and was given what seemed like an impossible mission. Japanese bombers were swarming like flies around the navel carrier the USS Lexington. Low on fuel and ammunition, Butch made four passes directly through the Japanese formation under heavy gunfire. The Japanese bombers were scattered and Butch made it back to the carrier. He not only saved the day but had shot down five Japanese planes and for his valor he was promoted to the rank of Lieutenant Commander. He also was the first U.S. serviceman in World War II and the first pilot ever to be decorated with the Medal of Honor. Butch, son of a Capone lawyer, became an instant celebrity. Though uncomfortable with all the fuss, parades and accolades followed him wherever he went. Sadly, in 1943, Butch led a squadron of night fighters and never returned home. At age 29, he died a hero serving his country. Butch's father Easy Eddie, would have been proud.

The invention of the mechanical rabbit lure for greyhound racing by Owen P. Smith may not only have influenced the eventual downfall of Al Capone and Easy Eddie and led to a 29-year old's early death as a fighter pilot in world II. It may also have been a pivotal invention that began the rise and fall of the "Sport of Queens" and the fading away of a wonderful dog that has served man for over 4000 years—the greyhound.

As for Easy Eddie's son Butch, his hometown tried to name a high school and a bridge after him but his mother wouldn't allow it because she felt all the troops were heroes. President Kennedy, who sought to end organized crime, was the one who finally succeeded in a memorial for Butch in 1963. So, the next time you fly in or out of Chicago's largest airport think about this story. Why? Because Easy Eddie's famous son was named Edward "Butch" O'Hare and Chicago's O'Hare International Airport bears their family name!

And for Al Capone a little lesson from the life it appears Easy Eddie was trying to live. Recognize your sins and attempt to make amends for your ways. After all, it is words from the Master.

O man, forgive thy mortal foe,
nor ever strike him blow for blow;
For all the souls on earth that live,
to be forgiven must forgive.

Forgive him seventy times and seven'
for all the blessed souls in heaven
Are both forgivers and forgive.

Alfred Lord Tennyson Adapted from—John W. DaisIII
in History and tagged Al Capone, Easy Eddie, Legal history,
O'Hare . . . 09/30/2015, and PUBLISHED OCTOBER 1,
2020, A version of this story appears in the March 2021 issue
of National Geographic magazine.

Thoughts on my Thoughts

San Francisco earthquake of 1989, also called Loma Prieta earthquake, was a major earthquake that struck the San Francisco Bay Area, California, U.S., on October 17, 1989, and caused 63 deaths, nearly 3,800 injuries, and an estimated $6 billion in property damage. It was the strongest earthquake to hit the area since the San Francisco earthquake of 1906.

I have this day imprinted on my mind as if it were yesterday:

- I remember being in an isolation room attending a sick dog infected with a new lethal virus infection telling my assistant not to drop the dog off the exam table. She did and I thought the dog was going to die. I remember the next day that the dog was miraculously not dying but beginning to recover from the disease.

- I remember the panic as to where my wife and children were and if they were safe.

- I remember my daughter with out of control fear because a bookcase at the top of our stairs at home fell over and just missed her as she was vacating the home during the earthquake. She asked me for a father's blessing to help her overcome her fear.

- I remember the day after day aftershocks. There was a depression in the road, Camden Avenue, in front of my hospital that whenever a large truck passed over it the earth under my feet felt like the aftershocks from the earthquake. The aftershocks worked on my nerves to the point where I wished we would have another earthquake and "get it over with" if that would stop them.

- I remember no cell phone or through the phone systems used at the time working. The only way we could use a landline was to plug in an old-style touch or rotary phone (if you had one) directly into the phone line at the circuit leaving the building.

- I remember Watsonville being isolated from outside services and volunteers using special equipment to reach them.

- I remember the concern I had for food & water, protection from the environment, looting, first aid available, getting out of the area if the roads became impassable, etc.

- I remember thinking about what I should do for my family to prepare for any disaster that may occur.

- I remember our church's response to try to get help to isolated areas.

- I remember dedicating each fifth Sunday Priesthood meeting to prepare for another disaster.

- I remember the organization of maps where members lived and individual assignments as to who we should check on if needed.

- I remember having meetings in our building and inviting people to see our demonstrations on food and water storage, first aid, items to have on hand, evacuation, and safety during a disaster, etc.

- I remember attending classes sponsored by the Red Cross learning CPR and other safety training.

- I remember attending a Ham Radio class and getting my license KD6KZI—I remember the number but as of this day I have no radio equipment and if I did, I would not know how to use it.

- I remember having a family meeting. The first order of business was on being safe in the home, where to meet if we got separated, and trying to calm the situation down and use our heads. Practice STOP—stop, think, observe and plan.

- I remember checking our bicycles to be sure each family member had one that they could use for getting around the area if the roads could not be used by vehicles.

- I remember going through our food items and getting items that had good storage and were easily prepared if needed.

- I remembered getting a water distiller in my garage that would make water that I placed in five-gallon containers for use at my work. This gave me a constant source of freshwater if it were needed. I always had at least 6 at home and would rotate them as they were used at work.

- I remember buying a home gas-operated generator. If the power was out it could be used to at least keep the refrigerator working.

- I remember filling backpacks with emergency supplies that could be quickly taken on our backs if needed on short notice. Also, emergency supplies were placed in the cars.

- I remember buying an RV and parking it alongside our home. It was loaded with clothing that would fit our family, first aid supplies, cash, food, water, other items that you would have in your home and kept full of fuel in case of an emergency. My thought was it could be used to "get out of Dodge", a place we could "hunker down", or full of supplies in which we could help the neighbors if necessary.

- I remember now my thoughts—now that I am an old man and my children are all safely nestled in their own homes that I am in hopes that when the big one comes that I would immediately be swept through the veil and not have to care anymore for this withered disaster struck temporal temple (my body). Recently we had our electricity shut off by PGE to prevent wildfires—

- I remember how poorly I was prepared to survive a few days of early darkness, cold, and lack of working emergency supplies. Even flashlights had to be scrambled for.

- I remember how great it is that we have our cell phones (that know almost anything we need or think we need), Amazon.com for supplies, and stores nearby that had their electricity on.

- I remembered how it does take frequent charges to keep our cell phones as smart as they are.

- I remember how after a couple of days without electricity my nerves began to get frazzled much like when I was experiencing the earthquake. I even noticed it affecting my son and his family who at first thought it would be fun "camping out" with the family.

Why do I bore you with all these remembers?

Several weeks ago, in a priesthood meeting, during a discussion on ministering needs my thoughts were, "If ye are prepared ye shall not fail." My thought was how many of us are prepared to take care of our family if a disaster occurred like I went through with my family?

- Then the power shutoffs reminded me again of my experience with the earthquake I lived through and I began to think about how much more vulnerable we may be today when compared to our situation then. Almost everything is in the cloud. On my cell phone, I have my notes which contain passwords, banking app's, and all other whatever's; my calendar has all my scheduled events, appointment times complete with a map available; my texts keep me abreast of family or work needs; my emails or safari gives me access to the "everything" and my treasured photos I've never saved take up a lot of memory.

- What would happen if we really had one of our favorite movie crises of complete loss of the cloud? Do we even have a plug-in landline phone that would work? I'm even told that if we had one of those EMP's (Electromagnetic Pulse) from a nuclear explosion it could cover an entire continent and cripple tiny circuits inside modern electronics on a massive scale. The power grid, phone and internet lines, and other infrastructure that uses metal may also be prone to the effects, which resemble those of a devastating geomagnetic storm.

On Monday, December 2nd, ten days after writing "Thoughts on My Thoughts," on a flight from Boise Idaho to San Jose I met a young man (he had a four and a nine-year old child) on his way to build a cell tower in Nevada for phone service. We got to talking and discussed the letter I have written to you about my concerns for disaster preparation. He told me that the cell towers currently being built are rated to withstand a 9.0 earthquake. However, the primary concerns are what will happen to the infrastructure that has been built to support cell tower transmissions. The major components of information technology (IT) infrastructure are the physical systems such as hardware, storage, and the building itself, networking, software, and any kind of routers/switches + the energy to support the systems (electricity). He mentioned that if there were any major disaster damaging the infrastructure we are in a "heap of trouble." He feels that we are too complacent and rely too heavily on our cell phone technology. In his personal life, he wants hard copies of any important items including bank transactions, important papers (insurance etcetera), and even his tax returns. He also feels that we could easily be in worse shape than we were in the 1989 earthquake simply because we rely too much on technology and most of us have prepared little to care for our family when disaster strikes.

- Remembering the remembering of my life has gotten me to think about getting a little better prepared. I can't count on the good Lord taking me right through the pearly gates or through the veil. I should suspect finding myself without access to a phone, heat, lights and wondering what will be next as I take the last of my prescription medications.

- I think that may be good advice for "you all's" too. So, as a parting gift, your son's Cub Master is giving you a copy of a handout called "Emergency Supplies for Earthquake Preparation"—or any disaster that may come as a surprise in your family's life. Thank you for putting up with me these last few years. I want to let you know that the experience I have had with the Cubs has helped make me a better old man . . . Thoughts on My Thoughts, written as a retiring Cub Scout Master for the parents during a disaster prevention pack meeting, *Walter R. Hoge, 11-23- 2019.*

"Prepare every needful thing and if you are prepared ye shall not fear . . ." D&C 88:119, 38:30

Life Is A Beach—If You Stay On The Beach—

On Valentine's Day 2021 I had just retired to bed when my son Jeremy informed me that there was a fire on our property and his family had heard two loud "booms" just before the fire was noticed. Investigating, from our bridge we saw a car turned over and burning on the side of the road about six feet from our mailbox on McKean Road. Firefighters were investigating the area from the road to the creek. During that night I wondered "how in the world" could anyone have allowed this accident to occur? On McKean Road, there is not a sharp curve coming from the north towards the property, and going south the road is straight with a 30 to 40 percent incline grade towards Calero Reservoir. During the night and early the next morning, my mind thought about all the negative things people might do that would result in such an accident. I even thought about what Forest Gump might have said, "Stupid is as stupid does." The next week several events gave me a mighty change of heart. Mosiah 5:2

On my way to work the day after the accident I noticed that someone had placed a vase full of beautiful flowers near the site of the accident. I was touched, my Adam's Apple was in my throat and my eyes were moist. That night I found an article about what was known about the crash. "SAN JOSE, CA—A 68-year-old Milpitas woman was one of the two people killed in a head-on accident Sunday evening in San Jose. The accident happened around 9:17 p.m., February 14, 2021, on McKean Road south of Schillingsburg Avenue. According to the California Highway Patrol, an unidentified man was driving a 2002 Chrysler southbound on McKean Road. For unknown reasons, he veered off the roadway and crossed over the double yellow lines into the northbound lane. The Chrysler then collided head-on with a 2008 Toyota where both occupants suffered fatal injuries and died at the scene. The cause of the crash is still under investigation."

My mind immediately reversed from the accident to a trip my family and friends took to Ensenada Mexico when my children were in their teens. We camped on the beach in tents and RV's enjoying the gentle waves and the warm ocean. One day several of us adults decided to swim across a calm area of the ocean to a sand bar and get away from the kids and the people lining the beach. We got over to the sand bar and a little later noticed the tide was coming in and decided it was time to swim back to the shore. We soon realized that the tide's current was pulling us towards the ocean. Fortunately, most of the women with us had kickboards to help them stay afloat. Even with the boards one of the strong swimmers in our group had to swim out to a couple of the ladies and help them get to shore.

A few days later we noticed several wave runners speeding along the beach just beyond the breakers and a helicopter circling around the area. It had not been long before we saw lifeguards pulling a man onto the beach. A group of people congregated around the body. I noticed that some of the young men we were with started making comments about what they conceived had happened. The words like drinking, stupid decision, couldn't swim etcetera came out of their mouths. I was angered and made them walk down the beach with me and get close enough to see what was going on. I remember the man looked middle age, in good health, and had a large gold chain around his neck. The youth found loving family members grieving the loss of one that was close to them. It didn't matter what had happened, this man was one of God's children and he would be missed by many people for the rest of their lives.

As my thoughts returned to the accident on Valentine's Day and I realized that I must not have taught myself the lesson I was trying to teach those teenage boys many years ago. I was also reminded that seemingly insignificant split second decisions can have lifelong or eternal ramifications.

Elder Larry A. Kache shared a similar incident during General Conference in 2014. "Brothers and sisters, the decisions we make in this life greatly affect the course of our eternal life. There are both seen and unseen forces that influence our choices. This point was brought home some five years ago in a way that almost cost me dearly. We were traveling with family and friends in the south of Oman. We decided to relax on the beach along the coast of the Indian Ocean. Soon after our arrival, our 16-yearold daughter, Nellie, asked if she could swim out to what she thought was a sandbar. Noticing the choppy water, I told her that I would go first, thinking there might be dangerous currents. After swimming a short while, I called to my wife, asking if I was close to the sandbar. Her response was, "You have gone way past it." Unbeknownst to me I was trapped in a riptide and was being pulled rapidly out to sea. I was unsure what to do. The only thing I could think of was to turn around and swim back toward shore. That was exactly the wrong thing to do. I felt helpless. Forces beyond my control were pulling me farther out to sea. What made matters worse was that my wife, trusting my decision, had followed me. Brothers and sisters, I thought there was a high likelihood I would not survive and that I, because of my decision, would also cause my wife's death. After great effort and what I believe was divine intervention, our feet somehow touched the sandy bottom and we were able to walk safely back to our friends and daughter." By *Elder Larry S. Kache, Of the Seventy, 'Trifle Not with Sacred Things', General Conference Oct 2014, Church of Jesus Christ of Latter-Day Saints.*

There are many currents in this earthly life—some safe and others not. President Spencer W. Kimball taught that there are powerful forces in our own lives much like the unseen currents of the ocean. These forces are real. We should never ignore them. To emphasize further by analogy the dangers of flirting with risky behavior, there is an oft-told story (the stagecoach principle) of three men who applied for the job of driving the stagecoaches for a transportation company. The successful applicant would be driving over high, dangerous, and precipitous mountain roads. Asked how well he could drive, the first one replied: "I am a good, experienced driver. I can drive so close to the edge of the precipice that the wide metal tire of the vehicle will skirt the edge and never go off." "That is good driving," said the employer. The second man boasted, "Oh, I can do better than that. I can drive so accurately that the tire of the vehicle will lap over, half of the tire on the edge of the precipice, and the other half in the air over the edge." The employer wondered what the third man could offer, and was surprised and pleased to hear, "Well, sir, I can keep it just as far away from the edge as possible." It is needless to ask which of the men got the job. *Spencer W. Kimball, 'The Miracle of Forgivenes'1969, pp 217-218.*

From time to time I have an image that haunts me. What if that September day, while relaxing on the beach of the Indian Ocean, I had said to my daughter Nellie, "Yes, go ahead. Swim out to the sandbar." Or if she too had followed my example and had been unable to swim back? What if I had to live life knowing that my example resulted in her being pulled by a riptide out to sea, never to return? Elder Larry S Kache

Proverbs 27:12 The prudent sees danger and hides himself, but the simple go on and suffer for it.

Gullible Gulls

"In our friendly neighbor city of St. Augustine, great flocks of seagulls are starving amid plenty. Fishing is still good, but the gulls don't know how to fish. For generations, they have depended on the shrimp fleet to toss them scraps from the nets. Now the fleet has moved.

. . . "The shrimpers had created a Welfare State for the . . . seagulls. The big birds never bothered to learn how to fish for themselves and they never taught their children to fish. Instead, they led their little ones to the shrimp nets. "Now the seagulls, the fine free birds that almost symbolize liberty itself, are starving to death because they gave in to the 'something for nothing' lure! They sacrificed their independence for a hand-out. "A lot of people are like that, too. They see nothing wrong in picking delectable scraps from the tax nets of the U.S. Government's 'shrimp fleet.' But what will happen when the Government runs out of goods? What about our children of generations to come? "Let's not be gullible gulls. We . . . must preserve our talents of self-sufficiency, our genius for creating things for ourselves, our sense of thrift, and our true love of independence." *"Fable of the Gullible Gull," Reader's Digest, Oct. 1950, p. 32.*

Seagulls are very intelligent. They have complex and highly developed communication skills ranging from vocalizations to body movements. They learn, remember and even pass on behaviors, such as stamping their feet in a group to imitate rainfall and trick earthworms to come to the surface, dropping hard-shelled mollusks onto rocks so that they break open to eat, following plowed fields where they know upturned food sources will be plentiful, and hovering over bridges to absorb raising heat from paved roadways. Seagulls pair for life and are attentive and caring parents. They take turns incubating their eggs, feeding and protecting the chicks. Young gulls form nursery flocks where they will play and learn vital skills for adulthood. Nursery flocks are watched over by a few adult males and these flocks will remain together until the birds are old enough to breed. Seagulls have a special pair of glands right above their eyes which flush salt from their body through openings in the bill. This allows them to drink both fresh and saltwater. A small claw halfway up their lower leg enables them to sit and roost on high ledges without being blown off. In Native American symbolism, the seagull represents a carefree attitude, versatility, and freedom. *OneKindPlanet, UK, 2016.* Seagulls are fondly remembered in Utah for helping Mormon settlers deal with a plague of crickets. The seagull is now the state bird of Utah and a monument in Salt Lake City commemorates the event, known as the 'Miracle of the Gulls'. The year

1848 was the Saints' second in the Salt Lake Valley and their first real chance at a full harvest. Following a mild winter, they optimistically planted a few thousand acres of crops in the spring. Double trouble arrived in late May, including deadly frost by night and insatiable hordes of crickets by day. Eliza R. Snow recorded: "This morning's frost in unison with the ravages of the crickets for a few days past produces many sighs, and occasionally some long faces." "Quite cold and very dry. Crops begin to suffer for want of rain," Isaac Haight wrote. "The crickets destroyed some crops and are eating the heads off the grain as soon as it heads out. The prospects for grain are discouraging." Historian William Hartley wrote, "When sticks, brooms, and clubs didn't keep the black creatures away, the weary pioneers attempted to drown the crickets. They tried to drive them into a fire. They went into the fields with bells and tin pans to scare them with noise. A 5-year-old girl was given a wooden mallet to smash crickets. A pair of brothers tried pulling a rope across the top of the crops to knock the crickets off. Ultimately, they "prayed and fought and fought and prayed," Hartley wrote. Around June 9th a pioneer named John Smith wrote that birds appeared every day for about three weeks. "There must have been thousands of them. Their coming was like a great cloud. When they passed between us and the sun, a shadow covered the field. I could see gulls settling for more than a mile around us." The pioneers marveled to find lumps of vomited crickets as the gulls gorged themselves to capacity, drank water, regurgitated, and continued to feed. Henry Bigler, a member of the Mormon Battalion, had just come from California to the Salt Lake Valley when he heard the news. On Sept. 28, 1848, he wrote of the Miracle of the Gulls: "The whole face of the earth I am told was covered with large black crickets that seemed to the farmers that they would eat up and completely destroy their entire crops had it not been for the gulls that came in large flocks and devoured the crickets. A Godsend, indeed. All acknowledged the hand of the Lord was in it, that He had sent the white gulls by scores of thousands to save their crops."

Hartley summarized his research on the Cricket War with other clarifying points, including Frost, crickets, and drought all contributed to serious crop damage in 1848. The gulls, natural enemies of the crickets and other insects, only helped with the crickets. The gulls were not strangers to Utah and they habitually regurgitate. The event was not clearly recognized by the LDS faith's First Presidency, its England newspaper, The Millennial Star, or those who wrote about the cricket infestation. The older a story gets, the more sensational it becomes. Harper said, "This is just how stories happen in folk culture, especially miracle stories. There's nothing really unusual about the story. Having said that, I don't mean to imply there's nothing providential about the story." The primary evidence from the time indicates the seagulls appeared, but their intervention was not as dramatic as it may have initially appeared. This does not invalidate the story, Griffiths said. "The gulls did appear, on a smaller scale than we sometimes envision, and that was a miracle to many of the early pioneers." *Was the "Miracle of the Gulls" Exaggerated? LDS Historians Explain, by Trent Toone, for LDS Living | Jul. 23, 2018.*

Seagulls are sanitation engineers with wings. The California Gulls scavenge large amounts of dead animals and organic litter which could pose a health threat to humans. There's been discussion about gulls at the San Francisco Giants' baseball games. Seems that during the seventh inning hundreds of gulls start to gather around the park, circling above the field and sitting on various perches around the stadium. The gulls have learned that there is a lot of food left in the park by fans dropping what remains of their Willie McCovey Pulled Pork Sandwiches and equally overpriced popcorn. Some have speculated that the birds are enticed by the smell of garlic fries but it's more likely that the enormous amount of wasted food was discovered visually by a few birds and the word got out. Why the seventh inning? The birds have learned that the noise, the commotion, and the singing of "take me out to the ballgame" signal the beginning of the departure of the fans and opening the opportunity to enjoy the cornucopia of leftover delights. Some people are complaining, even suggesting that the Giants should hand out BB guns or super soakers at the turnstiles instead of bobbleheads. *7X7 Editors, "Ask the Vet SF SPCA" March 25, 20211 & other.*

Not long after my family moved to California I had the opportunity to fish in the Pacific ocean for the first time. A friend and I decided to go to the Half Moon Bay Pier because it was nearby, we did not need to have special fishing gear and the cost to fish there was easily within both our budgets. We positioned ourselves on rocks that make up part of the pier and cast our bait into the bay. On my first cast, a seagull caught my bait attached to a hook in midair and flying away broke the line. I don't know what happened to the gull. Hopefully, its fate wasn't a hook stuck in a spot that resulted in starvation. This incident, the teaching of young seagulls how to find food effectively from a shrimp fleet's waste, and the San Francisco seventh inning stretch "Take Me out to the Ball Game" song attracting gulls to clean up the garbage sounds pretty smart to me. If there is a gullible party it's probably the human animal. The material left for consumption by the seagulls should also have value to us if we would just use some ingenuity like the gulls. Seagulls make the effort every day just to survive, find food to feed themselves and their young, and profiting from any opportunity that comes their way. As for the "Miracle of the Gulls" story history is almost always much more complicated than the clean stories that we repeat to each other. Harper said, "As a historian, I'm interested in how the Saints at the time understood the Cricket War. What did it mean to them there and then? There are letters and journal entries that show that they thought it was providential. They thought the Lord intervened and sort of turned the tide."

Marion G Romney taught that "all of our Church and family actions should be directed toward making our children and members self-reliant." He also states that becoming self-reliant is wonderful but it is only the means to an end. Self-reliance allows for greater freedom, but then what we do with that greater freedom is the true test. We must make the right choices by serving others and helping them to become self-reliant. Once the others also become self-reliant, they can serve and bless the lives of others and the cycle of service continues." The saying "Each one teach one" is an African proverb that originated in America during slavery times. Slaves were seen as chattel and therefore denied an education so when one slave learned to read or write, it became his duty to teach someone else. Frank Laubach, a Christian missionary went on to use the phrase to address poverty and illiteracy in the Philippines. It was later used in Jamaica to form the Adult Literacy Program. I remember hearing the phrase as a grade-school child learning about Mexico. Mankind learns by example, applying it in their daily lives and feeling the joy and satisfaction of being able to care for themselves and help others do the same. The California Gulls care for their young, protect and teach them behavior skills that will keep them safe and help them find the things necessary to survive on a daily basis. We raise our puppies by getting their attention from treat rewards, visual enforcement, and sounds of praise. The goal is to create a dependence and bonding to us and the satisfaction we have from living with something who greets us at the door, forgives and forgets, never has a bad day, and always has a smile expressed by the wag of the tail. To me, there's nothing much better than that.

To the gulls, it seems to be "each one teach one" and seeing nothing wrong in picking delectable scraps from a shrimp fleet, the San Francisco Giants stadium, or gleaning the fields of crickets. A lot of people are like that, too. "They see nothing wrong in picking delectable scraps from the tax nets of the U.S. Government's 'shrimp fleet.' But what will happen when the Government runs out of goods?

What about our children of generations to come? We . . . must preserve our talents of self-sufficiency, our genius for creating things for ourselves, our sense of thrift, and our true love of independence." And those of such good fortune should be prepared to use their time and talents to help care for the wellbeing, uplifting and teaching others success that are less fortunate than them. The 12th-century philosopher Maimonides wrote about eight degrees in the duty of charity. "The eighth he stated was the most meritorious of all, is to anticipate charity by preventing poverty, namely, to assist the reduced brother, either by a considerable gift or loan or money, or by teaching him a trade, or by putting him in the way of business, so that he may earn an honest livelihood and not be forced to the dreadful alternative of holding up his hand for charity."

Strive to be like the plants and animals of the world
—they make every effort possible to survive each day.

"Each one teach one" how to use their talents to succeed,
have self-respect, and a joyful happy life.

"Give a man a fish, and you feed him for a day.
Teach a man to fish and you feed him for a lifetime."

Mrs. Dymond, Anne Isabella Thackeray Ritchie, 1885

And above all:

"Pray as though everything depended of God;
Act as though everything depended on you."
St. Ignatius of Loyola, 16th.

Balance

Borneo is a 44,432 square mile rugged island in Southeast Asia. It has a population of 24 million people, is known for its beaches and ancient, biodiverse rainforest, and is home to wildlife including orangutans and clouded leopards. In the 1950s, the World Health Organization sent supplies of DDT to Borneo to fight mosquitoes that spread malaria among the people. The mosquitoes were quickly wiped out. But billions of roaches lived in the villages, and they simply stored the DDT in their bodies. One kind of animal that fed on the roaches was a small lizard. When these lizards ate the roaches, they also ate a lot of DDT. Instead of killing them, DDT only slowed them down. This made it easier for cats to catch the lizards that are one of their favorite foods. About the same time, people also found that hordes of caterpillars had moved in to feed on the roofing materials of their homes. They realized that the lizards that previously had kept the caterpillar population under control had been eaten by the cats. And now, all over North Borneo, cats that ate the lizards died from DDT poisoning. Then rats moved in because there were no cats to control their population.

With the increased rat population came increased health issues including concerns of the plague. Because of the intervention of man on the environment nature on Borneo was out of balance.

DDT was developed as the first of the modern synthetic insecticides in the 1940s. It was initially used with great effect to combat malaria spread by mosquitoes, typhus spread by fleas, and other insect-borne human diseases among both military and civilian populations. It also was effective for insect control in crop and livestock production, institutions, homes, and gardens. World War II was the first U.S. war in which diseases—many like typhus and malaria—killed fewer people than bullets and bombs. The reason was DDT. Hundreds of thousands of U.S. soldiers were issued DDT powder and told to sprinkle it in their sleeping bags. Entire towns in Italy were dusted with DDT from the air to control lice. DDT was sprayed heavily on South Pacific islands to control mosquitoes. Word got back to the home front that this new miracle chemical was saving the lives of loved ones. DDT's quick success as a pesticide and broad use in the United States and other countries led to the development of resistance by many insect pest species. In the early 1960's I remember my father-in-law trying to stash away DDT, before it was taken off the market, for use on his farm. He mentioned it was not killing flies in the barnyard as well as it used to but it still had good uses. This was during the time Rachel Carson published a book (1962) called Silent Spring that stimulated widespread public concern over the dangers of improper pesticide use and the need for better pesticide controls. In 1972, the Environmental Protection Agency issued a cancellation order for DDT based on its adverse environmental effects, such as those to wildlife, as well as its potential human health risks. In September 2006, the World Health Organization declared its support for the indoor use of DDT in African countries where malaria remains a major health problem, citing that the benefits of the pesticide outweigh the health and environmental risks and should not be enough to upset the balance of nature in the areas DDT is being used. ***Written by Bill Ganzel, the Ganzel Group + others***

Bryan Dyson former CEO of Coca Cola discussing balancing our personal lives stated, "Imagine life as a game in which you are juggling some five balls in the air. They are Work, Family, Health, Friends, and Spirit and you're keeping all of these in the air. You will soon understand that Work is a rubber ball. If you drop it, it will bounce back. But the other four balls—Family, Health, Friends, and Spirit—are made of glass. If you drop one of these; they will be irrevocably scuffed, marked, nicked, damaged, or even shattered. They will never be the same. You must understand that and strive for it." Work efficiently during office hours and leave on time. Give the required time to your family, friends, physical and spiritual needs. Everyday challenges have a way of pushing aside the real important purposes of why we are here. Finding a balance between what seems important and pressing at the time and building what is important in the long run to create true joy and happiness at the end of the game is a lifelong juggling act. At my age, I'm statistically rapidly going into the dying stage of my life. As I look back over the years I've been very lucky to have had diversions and experiences that have kept me from never feeling "I forgot to live." At times I would wish to be done with a life phase but realized that the next phase would not be any easier.

Life of a guy that was dying to live:

- *First I was dying to finish high school and start college-*

- *And then I was dying to finish college and start working—*

- *And then I was dying to marry and have children—*

- *And then I was dying for my children to grow old enough so I could concentrate better on my work -*And then I was dying to retire—*

- *And now, I am dying . . . and suddenly I realize I forgot to live—*

Please don't let this happen to you. Appreciate your current situation and balance your life each day old friend

—During the time we make money we lose our health, and in an attempt to restore our health we lose our money— We live as if we are never going to die, and we die as if we never lived—Author unknown

"From the day we arrive on the planet and blink as we step into the sun,

There's more to be seen than can ever be seen and more to do than can ever be done.

Some say eat or be eaten and some say live and let live,

But all are agreed as they join the stampede that you should never take more than you give.

Some of us fall by the wayside and some of us soar to the stars,

And some of us sail through our troubles and some have to live with the scars.

There's far too much to take in here and more to find than can ever be found.

In the circle of life, it's the wheel of fortune, it's the leap of faith, it's the band of hope,

Till we find our place on the path unwinding in the circle, the circle of life." *Elton John, Tim Rice—Lion King.*

Borneo island's rat problem caused by unbalancing nature in the area was fortunately relatively easy to resolve. Officials sent out emergency calls for cats. The cats were sent in by airplane and dropped by parachute to help control the rats. Unfortunately, unbalancing our lives may lead to consequences that our effort in the present or future can't restore balance.

"There is no trifling with nature; it is always true, grave, and severe; it is always in the right, and the faults and errors fall to our share. It defies incompetency, but reveals its secrets to the competent, the truthful, and the pure." Goethe, J.W. von 1749-1832

"The four balls—Family, Health, Friends and Spirit are made of glass" . . . To make money we lose our health, and then to restore our health we lose our money . . .

We may live as if we are never going to die, and unfortunately die as if we never lived . . .

The Christmas Star

The year 2020 will be recorded by historians and remembered by many as the year of the COVID-19 Pandemic and a Christmas wish that it would hurry and go away. For me, there is one event this year that I will always remember as a bright and wonderful experience starting the evening of December 21, 2020. On this date, Jupiter and Saturn engaged in a close alignment known as their "great conjunction." It is called a "great" conjunction because to ancient sky watchers, these are the two slowest moving planets in the sky. Jupiter takes nearly 12 years to describe a full circle in the heavens, spending a year visiting each zodiacal sign in the sky, while Saturn takes 29.5 years to make one full trip around the sun. Because of their respective slow movement, conjunction, or—to the ancients—a "celestial summit meeting," was rather unusual. Such get-togethers happen, in most cases, about every 20 years on average. But, when Jupiter and Saturn got together in December of this year it was not simply a conjunction it was as NASA described the "Great Conjunction of 2020" and as being a Christmas Star.

On Dec. 21, we saw Jupiter and Saturn separated by just 6 arc minutes. That's equal to 0.1 degrees or about one-fifth the apparent width of the moon. This was probably not close enough to make the planets appear to merge into a single bright star (although some did see that if they removed their eyeglasses). But in any case, it was something exceedingly rare to see. How often do these two planets come as close as that? Some websites say it has been nearly 400 years, while others say it's been almost 800 years. Indeed, the last time these two planets appeared so close was on July 16, 1623, when they were only 5 arc minutes apart—that's 397 years ago. During this "great junction" the positioning of the two planets was not located where many could have noticed it. The last time most of the world's population had a favorable view of these two planets coming so close to each other was on March 5, 1226, when they were even closer together (just 2 arc minutes) compared to what we saw on Dec. 21.

On Dec. 21, 2020, Jupiter and Saturn appeared just one-tenth of a degree apart, or about the thickness of a dime held at arm's length, according to NASA. During the event, known as a "great conjunction," the two planets (and their moons) were visible in the same field of view through binoculars or a telescope. So, based on our calculations, these two planets came exceedingly close to each other and were visible on an average of once every 375 years.

Some have suggested this holiday season that these two planets might be a replica of the legendary Star of Bethlehem. One of the more popular theories for the "Christmas Star" was a series of conjunctions between

Jupiter and Saturn in 7 BC. For in that year Jupiter and Saturn met not once but three times that year (in May, September, and December).

The first conjunction (on May 29—visible "in the east" before sunrise) presumably started the Magi on their way to Bethlehem from the Far East. The middle conjunction (September 30) may have strengthened their resolve in the purpose of their journey, while the third and final conjunction (Dec. 5) occurred just as they arrived in Judea to meet with King Herod, who sent them on to Bethlehem to "go and search diligently for the young child." For the Magi, Jupiter, pacing back-and-forth with Saturn in 7 BC would certainly have been looked upon as something unique. Whether from an astrological point of view that one single "celestial summit meeting" might have been a significant enough sign in the sky for the Magi to begin their trek to Judea is unknown. *Joe Rao instructor and guest lecturer at New York's Hayden Planetarium.*

Personally observing the Great Conjunction of 2020 struck me with awe and gave me the calming assurance that our hopes and dreams for our families and the world are in the hands of one who loves and cares for our well-being . . .

Most All Animals Have A Sniffer

My father and I were relieving ourselves in a public restroom when he said, "do you smell that? If you do, you have inherited the gift of smelling asparagus urine from me." Later I learned that the culprit was aspargusic acid that within 15 to 30 minutes after eating the digested asparagus causes urine to give off sulfur byproducts that evaporate rapidly into the air giving off the unpleasant scent that may last for 14 hours. Depending on which study you believe 20% to 50% of people experience asparagus urine and other foods such as brussels sprouts, onions, and garlic have also shown to be linked to odd smelling urine in some people.

In the 1820s the famous naturalist John J. Audubon set out to prove that turkey vultures use their superior eyesight, rather than their nostrils, to find carrion. He stuffed a deerskin with grass and added clay eyes, sewed up the imposter, and placed it in a meadow with its legs in the air. He watched as a vulture swooped down on it. The duped bird ripped out the eyes and tore apart stitches, then flying away after failing to find any meat. Audubon later placed a dead hog, its carcass reeking of decay in the July heat, in a ravine and covered it with a brush. This time vultures circled but didn't descend. The results were "fully conclusive," he wrote. Vultures did not scavenge by smell.

Audubon's ego would've taken a hit had he lived to see Kenneth Stager put his findings to the test. In 1960 Stager, an ornithologist at the Los Angeles County Natural History Museum showed that turkey vultures prefer fresher carcasses, typically no more than four days old, to putrid ones like Audubon hid. Stager also identified the specific scent that drew vultures to carrion, with the help of natural gas engineers who told him they followed the birds to ruptured pipelines. Decomposing carcasses, it turns out, give off ethyl mercaptan, the same sulfurous compound added to natural gas so humans can sniff out a leak (and which gives asparagus eaters' urine that distinctive rotten-egg odor). Stager had shattered Audubon's theory. Hardly anyone noticed. It's not all that surprising that Audubon's erroneous claim has persisted for so long. Birds sport flashy plumage, sing melodic songs and perform dramatic mating rituals. Vision and hearing are obviously important. But smell? Birds don't have noses or sniff everything the way dogs do. They lack the vomeronasal organ that most mammals, amphibians, and reptiles use to detect odor particles. And the smelling equipment they do possess can be hard to find: Many species have microscopic olfactory bulbs, a structure in the forebrain that receives odor signals from the nasal cavity. *Nancy Averett: This story originally ran in the January-February 2014 issue of Audubon, "The Sniff Test."* If a California Turkey Vulture can smell decomposing carcasses from high in the sky it is not hard to imagine that most birds use this fifth sense of smell as well as the sixth sense of navigation called magnetoreception. Then, nor should it hard to imagine that juvenile salmon can smell using a process called olfactory imprinting. This has been found to be a powerful and ingrained sense that enables these fish to return to the exact stream of their birth for spawning after traveling thousands of kilometers in the ocean.

Arthur Davis Hasler is best known for his research on salmon's olfactory ability to imprint their natal stream odors. He often told the story about the 1946 genesis of this discovery when he was vacationing in the Wasatch Range of the Rocky Mountains of Utah, where he had spent much time as a boy. Hiking up a mountain, yet out of sight of his favorite waterfall, he suddenly had what he called a "déjà senti" experience which is defined as a very familiar feeling, only that it was forgotten for some time, but has now been recovered with an increased sense of satisfaction. In other words, they feel a bit more satisfied as if they have been seeking this for some time. He describes this experience, "As a cool breeze, bearing the fragrance of mosses and columbine, swept around the rocky abutment, the details of this waterfall and its setting on the face of the mountain suddenly leapt into my mind's eye." Among other things, these smells reminded him of childhood memories and of home. If smells could trigger such memories in a human, they must be at least as evocative for salmon, Hasler reasoned. This revelation led to a rich and productive series of experiments and field trials on olfactory and solar orientation in fishes. *Arthur Davis Hasler, Academy of Science, 2003, Biographical Memoirs: volume 82.*

The ability to smell is often overlooked unless one loses it. The loss of smell is common for upper respiratory infections such as the common cold or flu—or allergies like hay fever—to temporarily impair your sense of smell. Known medically as anosmia, the symptom also occurs in approximately half of COVID-19 pandemic cases. While around two-thirds recover within eight weeks, many are still affected by the loss of smell. Often, people with COVID-19 experience loss of taste as a consequence of their loss of smell. Losing your sense of smell and taste can have a profound effect on your quality of life. As well as obvious dangers, being unable to smell expired food, or detect gas or smoke, there are emotional and practical effects. In a study co-authored by Professor Philpott at the University of East Anglia, the team found that almost every area of life is disrupted by smell loss, from concerns about personal hygiene to a loss of sexual intimacy with partners. ‹About two-thirds of patients report depression or anxiety as a consequence of smell loss,’ says Professor Philpott. Among people who suffer long-term, ‘around one-third will report losing weight because they lose all interest in food,’ he says. ‘Another third report gaining weight, because they go out of their way to stimulate their senses by eating takeaways and comfort eating.’ Many report feelings of isolation, ‘because they feel a disconnect from the social ethos connected to eating, but also to memories,’ Professor Philpott continues. Smell loss can make it difficult to bond with loved ones, ‘particularly partners,’ he says. ‘Some people experience an inability to maintain relationships or to form new ones because of the subconscious connection through smell. *Professor Carl Philpott from the University of East Anglia's Norwich Medical School, Lost your sense of smell, Annie Hayes, 23/01/21.*

Visiting family in Idaho I was presented with Samantha an elderly Siamese cat that was not doing well. She was drinking lots of water, eating a fair amount, losing bodyweight, weak on her back legs and her breath smelled like fingernail polish remover. I encouraged that the pet be seen by a veterinarian and I would attend if they would not mention my occupation. During the visit, the veterinarian discussed his concern for the cat's health, recommended doing a battery of tests, and that the results would be available the next day. I then told the doctor that I was noticing a sweet smell from Samantha's breath and asked him if he couldn't do a quick test for sugar like diabetics can do. He did, diabetes was diagnosed on the spot and the cat could begin therapy awaiting lab results to see if there were any other health concerns. This doctor was not a bad practitioner. It is suspected by me that he just didn't carry the right genetic code to smell the sweet aroma of acetone (ketones being produced from too much fat metabolism). A human patient-nurse asked an MD, "The sense of smell is an important tool we use during the rapid triage exam. I cannot seem to be able to recognize the characteristic smell of diabetic ketoacidosis. Many of my peers can tentatively diagnose this condition immediately on speaking with the patient. For some reason, I cannot smell it. I don't have problems with using my nose to detect other common diagnostic issues . . ." The doctor's reply was "that the ability to detect the odor of acetone on a patient's breath is genetic. I don't know whether it is dominant or recessive." *The Naked Scientists, why can't I smell diabetic ketoacidosis?* There is still debate about what gives one this ability to smell but I'll bet that when you look at the whole picture it will be credited to our genes.

Nearly five weeks ago (September 2021) my wife and I heard a scratching noise in our closet that appeared to be coming from the dresser drawers. We suspected a varmint but could not find it or any signs of nesting, droppings, or littered food items. We set a couple of peanut-baited traps in the dresser area without any success and the scratching noise disappeared after a few days. I could not see any signs in the attic and we assumed that the little critter must have been in the wall. About two weeks later I walked into our bathroom adjacent to the closet and when I turned on the lights found flies all over the ceiling and light fixtures. They were larger than house flies and easier to kill with a fly swatter. After several days they stopped showing up and I calculated that I had killed over thirty flies. Time passed with no more scratching to be heard or flies to swat. Then three days ago on a hot summer day, I walked into the closet and smelled a sulfurous rotten-egg smell coming from what I suspected to be decomposing carrion. At that moment I had a "deja senti" moment recalling something from the past that was very familiar to me. Not like Arthur Hasler's, "As a cool breeze, bearing the fragrance of mosses and columbine," but one of the of sulfurous rotten-egg gas produced from decomposing rats in the wall of my garage. They had been killed by a poison I used called Coumadin that is an anticoagulant blood thinner. The same compound is used by a lot of us older folks (called warfarin and taken in smaller quantities) to help prevent strokes and heart attacks. There must have been lots of rats, nesting material, droppings, and littered food items in that wall because it took months for the smell to finally go away. Maybe like Audubon's experiment using putrid hogs I didn't see California Turkey Vultures swooping over my home smelling carrion because the varmints were too decomposed. Here again, I believe I need to thank my parents for the gift of smell and thank them not so much for the gift of poor sight and hearing. I've needed my sense of smell to identify the dead varmints in the walls of my two homes, a natural gas leak from time to time, the smell of ketones on Samantha's breath and it's even okay for me to be reminded that I have recently eaten asparagus. However, I just hope my sugar A1C blood test values don't eventually rise high enough to enable my sniffer to find the sweet smell of acetone (ketones) from a diabetic on my breath.

The Manchester Terrier

In 2021 my family added a new member to our family by the name of B.B. after the color of our Ford Explorer. We were in the Ford showroom discussing the purchase of 2010 highly discounted Explorer, Kevan the salesman was telling us that the 2011 model coming out had much better gas mileage and my wife Shauna was gazing at a poster on the wall behind the salesman's head of a beautiful dark blood red color (Bordeaux) paint on a new Explorer. Shauna mentioned how beautiful the car looked, I liked the gas mileage sales pitch and we ordered the car to be built in Detroit Michigan. Being both parents and grandparents we started having fun sharing emails with the salesman and Ford Motor Company as if we were adopting a child. What seemed to be long-awaited progress reports on the manufacturing process—the life of the car began, hints here and there encouraged us that the car's production date would be met, and we were excited feeling all was well (kind of like a great ultrasound report of a fetus developing in an expectant mother). Shipment was announced and a delivery date was sent by email. Then it happened. The delivery date came and went. Our anxiety level rose after we felt we had waited longer than enough time and I called the Ford salesman. He made a few phone calls and informed us that our car could not be found. Approximately a week later a phone call came informing us that the Bordeaux painted Ford Explorer we had named Bridget Bordeaux (B.B.) was located in Salt Lake City and soon to be shipped to its intended birthing place, Nampa Idaho. Correspondence quotes from emails made just before receiving the car were: On 04/21/2011—Rich sent "Keep her diaper dry, fully bottle-fed and we should be able to be at the hospital on Sat. I'm so nervous I think I'll burn myself if I try to light up a cigar." Kevan's reply—"If it takes a while to finish hospital release forms etc . . . please throw in a couple of depends for the parents . . . Most grateful . . . I see the problem with Bridget. I received the permission slips for medical care, signed them, and plan to have them UPS'd today . . ." Rich—"No major problem. Just a clerical error by the hospital staff in charge of billing. Nothing to concern a new dad." "Presenting our special and lovely new 2011 addition, Bridget Bordeaux", April 29, 2011. An interesting thing I found out after we had named our recent new addition to our family B.B. is that the Brigitte Bardot did not spell her name the same as our Explorer or B.B.'s. She was born 09/28/1934 and often is referred to by her initials B.B. She is a French animal rights activist, former actress, and singer, she was one of the best-known sex symbols of the late 1950s and 1960s and she withdrew from the entertainment industry the year I graduated from veterinary school in 1973.

Our new family addition is a black and tan colored short-haired dog known as a Manchester Terrier that was first bred in Manchester England back in the 19th century to control vermin—mostly rats. The breed's claim to fame was its use in the sport called the "Rat Pit", a popular pastime of the 1800s that involved a 6-foot-wide circular pit riddled with rats. Dogs were dropped in and timed to see how many rats they could catch and kill while city dwellers gambled away their hard-earned shillings. Rat Pits, as disgusting as they sound, were found pretty much in every large town or city in England. Also, at the same time hunting rabbits with the small dogs was quite a popular sport. A five and a half pound English Toy Terrier Rat Pit Dog, closely related to the Manchester Terrier, named Terrier Tiny the Wonder was famous in the City of London in the mid-19th century for being able to kill 200 rats in an hour in the city's rat-baiting pits. At the time, the world record for killing 100 rats was 5 minutes, 30 seconds, held by a bull and terrier named Billy. At Bunhill Row in the City of London, a challenge for Billy's record was made for Tiny. Since they were healthier than London sewer rats, rats were brought from Essex for the rat pits located under a pub. They would bring in as many as 2,000 rats per contest. Tiny represented himself up for the challenge and later in 1848 & 1849 killed 200 rats in an hour having on both occasions time to spare. Terrier Tiny the Wonder was so small that he wore a woman's bracelet instead of a collar and once held the rat killing record, with 300 dead in just under 55 minutes. *The Manchester Terrier: A Scrappy, Loyal, Rat-Catching Super Dog, Alex Watson, 12/29/2020 & Wikipedia.*

Karen Brown, client of Camden Pet Hospital and friend, at the age of twelve fell in love with the Manchester Terrier. Her mother had taken away one of her pets and she defiantly went out and found another dog. B.B.'s mother, Sassy, had a life-threatening infection from slow-growing tuberculosis-like bacteria called Mycobacterium between her shoulder blades that was thought to have entered her body when an identification microchip was placed under the skin. After surgery and months of treatment, she recovered enough to be able to become a champion in the show ring and have two litters of puppies. Mrs. Brown's male Beau Petit, also a champion, was not interested in mating Sassy and her mating times were predicted by hormone tests and vaginal cytology. She then was impregnated by artificial insemination. Our family is very pleased that one of the eight puppies produced by Sassy's two litters has come our way.

By the end of the Second World War, there were only 11 Manchester Terriers registered with the Kennel Club and the breed was, and still is, classed as a vulnerable native breed. Just 164 births were registered in 2016. Manchester's best friend reached the height of its popularity in Victorian times where it got the nickname 'Gentleman's Terrier', now they have become pretty popular in America with a whole list of puppies looking for their forever homes on the American Kennel Club. Watching our ten-week-old vulnerable native breed Manchester Terrier with a face that looks like a baby flying fox bat is interesting. She is rapidly showing all the typical terrier behaviors of brave, mischievous, energetic, active, fearless, independent, playful, cheerful, and won't quit spirit during bloodless battles with her sister Abbie. I can't imagine how many rats over the century confronted this beautiful, vermin killing machine and lost. I also thought about how many lives had been saved from the Bubonic (Black) Plague spread by fleas that infected rats and man.

B.B. is taking over our hearts and a lot of our time. Her independence and hearing her name and coming when called are so far directed in her interests at the time. Her famous, rat killing, human health, and life-saving parental lines have recently come into question. In 2015 professor Nils Christian Stenseth and scientists from the University of Oslo said they've compared tree-ring records from Europe and Asia with more than 7,000 outbreaks of the plague. They conclude that weather during much of that period would be too wet for rats to flourish and carry infected fleas across continents. But he says wet springs succeeded by warm summers would be a honeymoon atmosphere for another species of vermin. «Such conditions are good for gerbils,» Stenseth told the BBC. "It means a high gerbil population across huge areas, and that is good for the plague. "If we're right," he added, "we'll have to rewrite history." Gerbils may be the real rats and the Manchester Terrier and their relatives may have only helped reduce the spoiled and lost food caused by the rats at that time. Maybe the Gerbils did it and maybe there are better cars than the 2011 Ford Explorer—but in our lives, we still believe in our two B.B.'s

*"We spent many a day preparing and
planning for her to come our way.
And we're so impressed we've asked her to stay:
Our first impression was, "We like what we see,
Because she's as pretty as any car (or dog) could be."
She'll be around to help us explore and to play:*

*As we find free time (at home or)
to get far, far away . . .*

*"Presenting our special and lovely new
2011 addition, Bridget Bordeaux (B.B.),"
and April 29, 2021's new B.B.*

Oh Pizzle Sticks

The other day I found one of the best things for my puppy that loves to chew and chew. The treat keeps the dog's attention and it takes time to be consumed. The name is pizzle or bully stix (stick) and the ones I bought were made in the USA. They are made from beef and a supplier named Ryan described how sticks are made. "In March 2019, I went to visit my suppliers in Colombia. I am really proud of the product they create. However, I haven't found a lot of transparency explaining the procedure used in making them. Here's my effort to change that. The process of making bully sticks is fascinating but because the industry wants to keep the process a secret from other potential producers, retailers don't know the process themselves, the industry may think it might scare off their consumers (I disagree with this), or another reason I'm not aware of. The raw product comes from the slaughterhouses where the cattle are processed. Manufacturers work with the slaughterhouses to take the beef byproducts to make sticks and other popular dog treats like ears, tails, hooves, etc. that the human meat industry has not traditionally had great demand for. They receive daily deliveries that are kept cold until ready to make the sticks by cleaning, trimming away the fat and fluids, soaking and washing, vertically hanging, stretching, and cooking until hardened to produce the long-lasting chewing product with a relatively long shelf-life. After cooking the sticks are called a canes and are typically 24" to 36" long. The large canes are then cut down to the size of 6" to 12" by using a bandsaw. The sticks are weighed, packaged, and shipped to be consumed by "man's best friend." ryan@bullybundles.com.

In 1994 I purchased a pizzle cane that had been made into a walking stick. It is beautiful in texture and the color of deep brown reminds me of my kitchen table. That year my family dressed like we perceived the Jewish population would have looked during the time Joseph and Marie with child walked nearly a hundred miles to satisfy Caesar Augustus' decree in Luke 2:1-6 that all the world should be registered. As I recall, the program was called "Back to Bethlehem" and we followed a donkey through part of the neighborhood until we arrived at the church where each family set up their tent in the cultural hall and sat on pillows. We participated in a Christmas program in preparation for the celebration of the birth of Christ. During the performance an elderly lady became intrigued by my walking stick and asked a lot of questions that considering what I knew about its source, my young age, being inside a church building and the spirit of the evening—I was too bashful to answer. "There are two kinds of bashfulness: One, the awkwardness of the booby, which a few steps into the world will convert into the pertness of a coxcomb (a silly, vain foppish fellow); the other, a consciousness, which the most delicate feelings produce, and the most extensive knowledge cannot always remove." *Mackenzie, Henry 1745-1831.* At the time I was more concerned at the awkwardness of the situation than thoughtful of the possibility of the "delicate feelings" I might produce. I also was lucky that she did not see so good and had not seen the information sticker about the origin of the walking stick. I'm sure my dog doesn't care about where the Pizzle Stix came from—but I'm not sure how our discussion would have changed if the woman had read the stickers on the walking stick:

You believe this is made from a bull's reproductive organ?
"The last of the old bull, the cause of it all!"
O'l Bull 417 858-2547. I haven't tried the phone number but in due time curiosity may prevail.

I meet weekly for an hour with a group of elderly gentlemen near my age. One of the wives named it ROMEOS (retired old men eating out single). One gentleman in his ninety's has a walking stick that has caught my eye and there is a great story about where it came from. Next Monday I'm going to take my pizzle cane to ROMEOS, see where the conversation goes and have some fun trying to exchange canes. Probably the lady that I showed my walking stick to in 1994 at the Christmas party would have had about the same conversation with me and in both cases I will probably be the one with the one red-faced and uneasy.

Life's Journey

The American Revolution was to some extent a fight over the big, stupid, slow-moving codfish. Codfish were by far colonial New England's biggest export. The codfish was so important to New England that John Adams made sure the British allowed U.S. fishermen access to the Grand Banks and other banks off Newfoundland as part of the Treaty of Paris. Adams believed the fledgling country needed a thriving fishery to have trained mariners who could serve in the navy. The U.S. Congress agreed with him, and in 1792 decided to pay fishermen a bounty for catching codfish. The codfish had special importance to Massachusetts, where to this day the wooden Sacred Cod hangs above the chambers of the commonwealth's House of Representatives. Between 1768 and 1772, fish accounted for 35 percent of all the money New England made overseas. Livestock came in a poor second, at 20 percent.

There is a story told that at the change of the century in the northeastern United States, codfish were considered not only delectable, they are also a very big commercial enterprise. A vast industry had grown up around catching, preparing, and shipping codfish to every part of the country. But the great demand for codfish posed a problem to the shippers. At first, they froze the codfish before shipping, but freezing them took away much of the flavor. Then they tried shipping the codfish alive in saltwater, but that didn't work either. Finally, someone hit on a creative solution. The codfish were placed in a shipping tank with their natural enemy—catfish. From the time the codfish left the east coast until they arrived at their destination, the catfish chased the codfish all over the tank! When they arrived, the codfish were as fresh as when they were first caught with no loss of flavor or texture.

All of us live in a "tank" and face the world's catfish on a regular basis. Some of these catfish causing adversity will be of our own making and others will be from the testing that a wise Heavenly Father determines is needed to help us grow, gain understanding and compassion which will polish us for our everlasting benefit. To get from where we are to where we need to be requires a lot of stretching, and that generally entails catfish causing discomfort and pain. *From Pastor Charles Swindoll, "God's Catfish", Elder Richard G. Scott, "21 Principles", other thoughts . . .*

For adults, the top ten most stressful life events and their *"Life Change Unit" scores established by the Holmes and Rahe Scale* are as follows: death of a spouse (or child): 100, divorce: 73, marital separation: 65, imprisonment: 63, death of a close family member: 63, personal injury or illness: 53, marriage: 50, dismissal from work: 47, marital reconciliation: 45 and retirement: 45. *https://paindoctor. com,*

Inside Pain Blog. These are events that all of us at one time or another will face during our lives. I have come to the conclusion that these events are there to help us understand who we are and what we can become. I think of the challenges Job faced during his life and the words that Joseph Smith was given when a prisoner in Liberty Jail in 1839 and received council. ". . . if thou shouldst be cast into the pit, or into the hands of murderers, and the sentence of death passed upon thee; if thou be cast into the deep; if the billowing surge conspires against thee; if fierce winds become thine enemy; if the heavens gather blackness, and all the elements combine to hedge up the way; and above all, if the very jaws of hell shall gape open the mouth wide after thee, know thou, my son, that all these things shall give thee experience, and shall be for thy good . . ." D & C: 7

Albert Camus stated, "In the depth of winter, I finally learned that within me there lay an invincible summer." I have found during my life that "Life is very interesting. In the end, some of your greatest pains become your greatest strengths." *Drew Barrymore* I wish to be like the plants and animals found on this earth that have the spirit to struggle to survive every moment of their lives and don't get depressed or discouraged. They just keep on keeping on until their life here ends.

I was a teenage lad in 1960 or sixty-one, staying in a cabin and having great fun. There was a clear fast-flowing creek near the place and I stopped off to rest, and as I leaned quietly on a tree stump, I noticed some shade on the creek and a trout constantly swimming just to stay in one spot.

And I thought to myself why do you make such an effort doing so much work and you'll just die one day. A thought I have had from time to time as fear and discouragement has come my way.

You have to swim all day and though there's an eddy of slower current you still need to swim. You can't even sleep or you'll float down the stream and probably be caught and eaten!

I noticed the trout investigating things that floated by—some it swallowed, some it placed in its mouth and quickly "spit it out" and some it got close to it investigated and then turned away.

The trout would hide in the shade or the eddy behind the rock, I noticed when it was in the sunny parts of the creek was where it found most of its food.

But if there was movement from a bird flying by, me, or a tree branch from a puff of wind, the trout darted for cover in the shady side of the creek.

I thought about what I saw realizing that this is nature's way, For all the plants and animals to survive without another thought from day to day.

And how God made them out of the reach of Lucifer when he was cast down to earth.

If mankind were like the trout and just would get away from bad things or when tried "spit them out", move away when in the limelight of danger and understand God and follow in His way.

We'd be closer to nature, that knows no sin, and when we pass on have God welcome us in.

Walter R. Hoge, "Just a Fish (Fable of a Trout)", 2021
"Life is not a journey to the grave with the intention of arriving safely in a well-preserved body, but rather to skid in broadside, thoroughly used up, totally worn out, and loudly proclaiming, "Wow what a ride!"

Hunter S. Thompson,
The Proud Highway:
Saga of a Desperate Southern Gentleman, 1955-1967

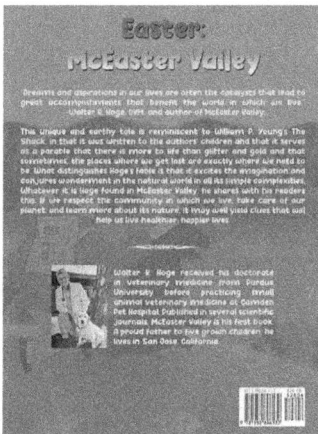

Author Biography

Walter R. Hoge received his master's degree and a doctorate in veterinary medicine from Purdue University before practicing small animal veterinary medicine. Currently and for the last forty-five years, he has practiced at Camden Pet Hospital. He has been published in several scientific journals and written a book called *Easter: McEaster Valley*. A proud father to five grown children and 17 grandchildren, he lives in San Jose, California.

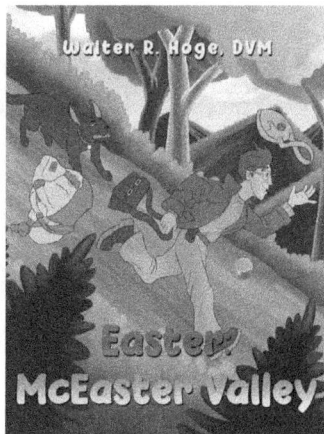

"Dreams and aspirations in our lives
are often the catalysts that lead to great accomplishments that
benefit the world in which we live."
-Walter R. Hoge, DVM, and author
of Easter: McEaster Valley

This unique and earthy tale is reminiscent of William P. Young's The Shack, in that it was written to the author's children and that it serves as a parable that there is more to life than glitter and gold and that sometimes, the places where we get lost are exactly where we need to be. What distinguishes Hoge's fable is that it excites the imagination and conjures wonderment in the natural world in all its simple complexities. Whatever it is Hoge found in McEaster Valley, he shares with his readers this: If we respect the community in which we live, take care of our planet, and learn more about its nature, it may well yield clues that will help us live healthier, happier lives. "Since visiting McEaster Valley, I have taken the supposed problems of the world a little less seriously. We are constantly striving to make our lives simpler but are, in reality, making them more complicated. When the push and stress get to be too much for me, I think of McEaster Valley and the order of nature and the innocent animals living their lives and accepting whatever comes their way by putting their best foot forward and going on. Most of us don't seem to realize that God made this earth and placed us on it so we could have joy and learn who we are before going on to the next estate." *-an excerpt from the book Easter: McEaster Valley by Walter R. Hoge, DVM*

Thoughts on My Thoughts: The <u>TALES</u> That Wagged This Veterinarian by Walter R. Hoge

Rating: Gold

A moving autobiography highlighting the author's life as a veterinarian and the joy he gets from serving others

Walter R. Hoge's *Thoughts on My Thoughts: The <u>TALES</u> That Wagged this Veterinarian* is an inspiring book that looks back at Hoge's childhood to him becoming a dedicated veterinarian. All throughout the book, Hoge never fails to inject humor as he shares memories of him growing up. Despite being a typical naughty child, Hoge transitioned and took his studies seriously. Being an animal lover, choosing which career path to take was easy for him.

Graduating top 10 in his class, Hoge began practicing veterinary medicine in 1973. Despite doing good in his class, Hoge realized and recognized that he still needs to learn more. He made it a point to observe the techniques of his older and experienced colleagues. By observing them, he soon learned the art of veterinary practice from his successful peers.

Hoge's memoir is not limited to his life as a veterinarian and his work and relationship with animals. He also recalls the sad and happy moments of his life. His ups and downs. He recalls how he took care of his wife who was dying from cancer, and the grief he felt when she passed away. He also shares the time when he had a stroke. These life events almost made him stop practicing veterinary medicine. But he never gave up and continued doing what he does best.

This book will also help aspiring veterinarians as Hoge shares information about medical conditions in animals and people. Hoge's dedication to his work is unparalleled and will inspire others. He discusses unconventional examples used in medical discussions. An example is when a veterinarian put mites in his ears to fully understand how to treat dogs for ear mites. Not all vets are brave enough to try this treatment style.

Thoughts on My Thoughts is uplifting and motivational. Some may think that a veterinarian's work is always easy when at times it's difficult. They may receive complaints and death threats when an animal isn't treated to a client's liking or dies in their care. Hoge experienced some of these, but his care for the animal and the joy of serving his clients far over shadowed whatever fear and danger he faced.

Thoughts on My Thoughts: The <u>Tales</u> That Wagged This Veterinarian

By Walter R. Hoge, DVM
ReadersMagnet

Book Review by Kate Robinson

> *"You can't always do much to change circumstances, so smile."*

Dr. Walter R. Hoge, DVM, shares his considerable experience as a veterinarian and as a kind and thoughtful human being in this delightful collection of autobiographical essays. Each chapter addresses a unique topic, or thematic set of memories, and the non-linear format is fresh and appealing, allowing readers to skip around and enjoy their favorite stories while being in the moment with this remarkable man.

Not all the essays are about Hoge's veterinary work, and many have a practical Christian foundation that is never heavy or overbearing. In fact, readers will discover that this blend of science and spirituality is harmonious and steeped in the wisdom that comes from both ends of a necessary spectrum. Some of the sundry, fascinating topics that Hoge addresses are reflected in chapter titles: "Procrastinate or Straightway," "Good Intentions Going Bad May Not Be So Bad," "Every Life Is a Wonderful Story," "Curse and Hate Letters," "Sunflowers and Life," "Divine Intervention," "No One Likes a Frowning Face," "Life As It Is," "Sugar Beets and Falling Off the Truck," and "Value of Failure," among many other topics. The more personal essays include titles such as "Our Elf On the Shelf Nearly Started a Fire," "Sheep vs. Goats," "Toothpaste On the Mirror," "Who Packed My Parachute," and "Greyhounds and Al Capone," among many other timely and timeless topics.

Hoge has a pleasing way of ping-ponging from the general to the specific and back again—a good sign of a lively writer with an inquiring mind and the ability to engage readers. It's a refreshing surprise throughout the book to discover where Hoge's mind and spirit have led him as he records his observations on paper. He includes some of his life experiences from boyhood and his coming of age and also reveals much about his veterinary training and forty-five-year career as a veterinarian. Of course, a busy family life with his wife and five children (and later, seventeen grandchildren) spark many reflections.

Hoge also reveals much about his commitments to his physical and spiritual communities. There are many moral lessons in Hoge's writing, and he delivers these fables and aphorisms, many of which are quite profound, with wry humor and a light touch. It feels as if there's hardly anything that the author hasn't thought about or managed to include in these pages, from his experiences raising pigeons in boyhood, working in a mental health facility in Idaho during his high school years, sketches about meeting and courting his future wife, and a plethora of other relatable incidents with both human and non-human beings, whether livestock, domestic pets, or those critters that live in the wild under nature's umbrella.

In one chapter, Hoge writes about the eminent American painter Norman Rockwell, and one can surmise that Hoge has a disposition much like Rockwell's: "Rockwell could have easily painted, as some say, 'life as it is.' He could have concentrated on scenes of his or others' sorrow and moments of misery. He might have painted the mean and nasty, the cruel and depraved." Instead, he notes, "Rockwell chose to look for the good, the kind, the simple and happy moments that make life worth living." Like Rockwell, Hoge has a pleasant and satisfying way of guiding readers along the path of his perspective and then leading them back home to reflect upon their own hearts. Plus, how can readers resist the lure of puppies and wallabies and ants and camels and sunflowers with the comfort of spiritual guidance along the way?

RECOMMENDED by the US Review

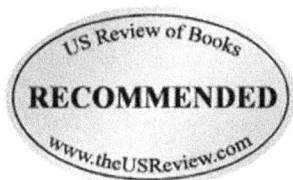

US Review of Books
RECOMMENDED
www.theUSReview.com